COMPREHENSIVE RESEARCH
AND STUDY GUIDE

BLOOM'S
MAJOR
DRAMATISTS

Aeschylus

EDITED AND WITH AN
INTRODUCTION BY HAROLD BLOOM

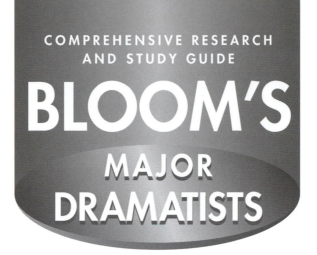

COMPREHENSIVE RESEARCH
AND STUDY GUIDE

BLOOM'S
MAJOR
DRAMATISTS

Aeschylus

EDITED AND WITH AN INTRODUCTION
BY HAROLD BLOOM

Introduction © 2002 by Harold Bloom.

Printed and bound in the United States of America.

First Printing
1 3 5 7 9 8 6 4 2

Library of Congress Cataloging-in-Publication Data
Aeschylus / edited and with an introduction by Harold Bloom.
        p. cm. —(Bloom's major dramatists)
    Includes bibliographical references and index.
    ISBN 0-7910-6355-0 (alk. paper)
    1. Aeschylus—Criticism and interpretation.   2. Mythology, Greek, in
    literature.   3. Tragedy. I. Bloom, Harold. II. Series.

    [PA3829 .A38 2001]
    882'.01--dc21   2001047591

Chelsea House Publishers
1974 Sproul Road, Suite 400
Broomall, PA 19008-0914

The Chelsea House World Wide Web address is
http://www.chelseahouse.com

Series Editor: Matt Uhler

Contributing Editor: Emmy Chang

Produced by Publisher's Services, Santa Barbara, California

Contents

User's Guide

This volume is designed to present biographical, critical, and bibliographical information on the author's best-known or most important works. Following Harold Bloom's editor's note and introduction is a detailed biography of the author, discussing major life events and important literary accomplishments. A plot summary of each play follows, tracing significant themes, patterns, and motifs in the work.

A selection of critical extracts, derived from previously published material from leading critics, analyzes aspects of each play. The extracts consist of statements from the author, if available, early reviews of the work, and later evaluations up to the present. A bibliography of the author's writings (including a complete list of all works written, cowritten, edited, and translated), a list of additional books and articles on the author and his or her work, and an index of themes and ideas in the author's writings conclude the volume.

$\sim$

Harold Bloom is Sterling Professor of the Humanities at Yale University and Henry W. and Albert A. Berg Professor of English at the New York University Graduate School. He is the author of over 20 books, including *Shelley's Mythmaking* (1959), *The Visionary Company* (1961), *Blake's Apocalypse* (1963), *Yeats* (1970), *A Map of Misreading* (1975), *Kabbalah and Criticism* (1975), *Agon: Toward a Theory of Revisionism* (1982), *The American Religion* (1992), *The Western Canon* (1994), and *Omens of Millennium: The Gnosis of Angels, Dreams, and Resurrection* (1996). *The Anxiety of Influence* (1973) sets forth Professor Bloom's provocative theory of the literary relationships between the great writers and their predecessors. His most recent books include *Shakespeare: The Invention of the Human,* a 1998 National Book Award finalist, and *How to Read and Why,* which was published in 2000.

Professor Bloom earned his Ph.D. from Yale University in 1955 and has served on the Yale faculty since then. He is a 1985 MacArthur Foundation Award recipient, served as the Charles Eliot Norton Professor of Poetry at Harvard University in 1987–88, and has received honorary degrees from the universities of Rome and Bologna. In 1999, Professor Bloom received the prestigious American Academy of Arts and Letters Gold Medal for Criticism.

Currently, Harold Bloom is the editor of numerous Chelsea House volumes of literary criticism, including the series BLOOM'S NOTES, BLOOM'S MAJOR DRAMATISTS, BLOOM'S MAJOR NOVELISTS, MAJOR LITERARY CHARACTERS, MODERN CRITICAL VIEWS, MODERN CRITICAL INTERPRETATIONS, and WOMEN WRITERS OF ENGLISH AND THEIR WORKS.

Editor's Note

This volume is concerned with the only surviving trilogy by Aeschylus, the *Oresteia,* which we are lucky to have, as of his four other extant plays, each is the lonely relic of a trilogy. But then the loss of most of Aeschylus's dramas would still be a cultural tragedy (he is thought to have composed some seventy to ninety) except that our current relationship to all the classics, from Homer to Joyce, is a cultural tragedy in the dumbed-down English-speaking world. Perhaps I should say "numbed-down," as I faithfully peruse all the instant classics of multicultural correctness, and find myself rendered numb.

My Introduction centers upon Clytemnestra, murderer of her husband, Agamemnon, who had sacrificed their daughter, Iphigeneia, in order to appease the goddess Artemis. Without this ghastly initial execution, the ships could not sail for Troy. How to interpret Clytemnestra's revenge is not an easy task in this trilogy of endless ambivalences.

Agamemnon, which begins the trilogy, has eleven critical views devoted to it in this volume.

H. D. F. Kitto leads off with a reminder that the play is dance-theater, after which Robert F. Goheen relates the carpet-scene of *Agamemnon* to the celebratory robes of the Furies at the reconciled close of the *Eumenides.* Froma Zeitlin comments on how the language of sacrificial slaughter is repeated throughout *Agamemnon.*

Deferred time, a curious feature of the *Agamemnon,* is seen by Jacqueline de Romilly as a function of divine justice, delayed, but certain, after which John J. Peradotto considers the imagery that implies Agamemnon's guilt at having sacrificed an innocent daughter in order to launch a fleet to recover an adulterous sister-in-law.

P. E. Easterling examines Agamemnon's yielding to hubris in the carpet-treading scene, while John Gould sees the characters of the play as being images rather than personalities.

Clytemnestra's metaphors are analyzed by Aya Betensky, who finds in them a destructive joy, after which Brooks Otis sees the play's characters as agents of transition, and Timothy Gantz doubts the relevance of inherited guilt to Aeschylus.

The seven extracts on *The Libation Bearers* begin with Anne Lebeck, who traces the significance of the play's invocation, while Brian Vickers outlines our increasing alienation from Clytemnestra.

The line-by-line exchanges are studied by Stanley Ireland, after which A. F. Garvie demonstrates the use of suspense by the dramatist.

Oliver Taplin shows the similarities in the murder-tableaux of Agamemnon and Clytemnestra, while A. L. Brown centers upon the madness of Orestes, and Marsh McCall discovers in the slave-chorus intimations of the drama's catastrophe.

The eight Critical Views on the *Eumenides* begin with my distinguished former teacher, Friedrich Solmsen, who emphasizes the role of the Court of Athens, the Areopagus, in resolving the conflicts of the trilogy.

George Thomson, a Marxist critic, considers the socio-political context of the play, after which Michael Gagarin examines the sexual conflict enacted in the final drama of the trilogy.

For Philip Vellacott, there is only irony in the resolution of the *Eumenides,* while D. A. Hester questions the vote that untangles the play.

Nancy S. Rabinowitz finds in the duality of the Furies a clue to their conversion, after which Thomas G. Rosenmeyer sees Aeschylus as contriving his gods as dramatic agencies, and Simon Goldhill shows the clash throughout the *Oresteia* of differing perspectives upon the term *dikē,* which only roughly means "just."

Introduction

HAROLD BLOOM

When Odysseus encounters the ghost of Agamemnon in the underworld (*Odyssey*, Book XI) the embittered shade memorably recalls his slaughter by his extraordinary wife:

> As I lay dying the woman with the dog's eyes would not
> close my eyes for me as I descended into Hades.

One recalls that Faulkner took the title for his most original novel from those first four words, but Aeschylus created an Agamemnon who is less imposing than Homer's. Selective in his use of the story, Homer omits any mention of the sacrifice of Iphigeneia by Agamemnon, and does not tell us that the Furies harried Orestes for his matricide. *The Odyssey* intimates that Clytemnestra was hateful, but does not elaborate. Aeschylus, who somehow gives me the uncanny notion that he is more archaic than Homer, certainly more primordial, portrays a Clytemnestra far more vivid than any other role in the *Oresteia*.

Clytemnestra's hatred for her husband appears to transcend his ritual sacrifice of Iphigeneia, and pragmatically represents a desire to usurp the kingdom. Aeschylus could not have been unaware of the negative splendor with which he had endowed Clytemnestra. One hesitates to call her a heroine-villain, though the mixed metaphor of lioness-serpent, mother of the lion Orestes whom she calls a serpent, certainly applies to her.

Since Clytemnestra is dramatically and imaginatively stronger than Agamemnon, his slave-mistress Cassandra, and the avenging Electra and Orestes, she certainly is the most memorable figure not only in the trilogy, but in all of Aeschylus that has survived. She is superbly flamboyant, and fascinates us because she exults outrageously in her slaughter of Agamemnon, and also in her wholly gratuitous butchery of the innocent Cassandra. I employ here the translation of Richmond Lattimore (1947), to give Clytemnestra's speech as she stands over the bodies of Agamemnon and Cassandra:

> Much have I said before to serve necessity,
> but I will take no shame now to unsay it all.

How else could I, arming hate against hateful men
disguised in seeming tenderness, fence high the nets
of ruin beyond overleaping? Thus to me
the conflict born of ancient bitterness is not
a thing new thought upon, but pondered deep in time.
I stand now where I struck him down. The thing is done.
Thus have I wrought, and I will not deny it now.
That he might not escape nor beat aside his death,
as fishermen cast their huge circling nets, I spread
deadly abundance of rich robes, and caught him fast.
I struck him twice. In two great cries of agony
he buckled at the knees and fell. When he was down
I struck him the third blow, in thanks and reverence
to Zeus the lord of dead men underneath the ground.
Thus he went down, and the life struggled out of him;
and as he died he spattered me with the dark red
and violent driven rain of bitter savored blood
to make me glad, as gardens stand among the showers
of God in glory at the birthtime of the buds.

These being the facts, elders of Argos assembled here,
be glad, if it be your pleasure; but for me, I glory.
Were it religion to pour wine above the slain,
this man deserved, more than deserved, such sacrament.
He filled our cup with evil things unspeakable
and now himself come home has drunk it to the dregs.

Few utterances in drama before Shakespeare have so stunning a
force. The third blow is a shocker, but less so than the image of the
murderess as gardens gloried by the rain of her husband's blood.
Even in Shakespeare's panoply of Lady Macbeth, Goneril, and Regan,
there is no woman of similar violence. To go beyond this might seem
unlikely, but Aeschylus surpasses it in Clytemnestra's sadistic delight
at having added Cassandra to the orgiastic slaughter:

Now hear you this, the right behind my sacrament:
By my child's Justice driven to fulfilment, by
her Wrath and Fury, to whom I sacrificed this man,
the hope that walks my chambers is not traced with fear
while yet Aegisthus makes the fire shine on my hearth,
my good friend, now as always, who shall be for us
the shield of our defiance, no weak thing; while he,
this other, is fallen, stained with this woman you behold,
plaything of all the golden girls at Ilium;

and here lies she, the captive of his spear, who saw
wonders, who shared his bed, the wise in revelations
and loving mistress, who yet knew the feel as well
of the men's rowing benches. Their reward is not
unworthy. He lies there; and she who swanlike cried
aloud her lyric mortal lamentation out
is laid against his fond heart, and to me has given
a delicate excitement to my bed's delight.

It is wonderfully clear that Clytemnestra's hatred for Agamemnon is sexual, a woman's resentment of a male weaker than herself, who rules over her only because of gender. Her pride in her double-murder is exuberant, and her hatred extends both to Zeus and to Cassandra. Ironically extending reverence to Zeus as "lord of dead men underneath the ground," she implies a hatred towards him as well, presumably as supreme male. But why does she relish her murder of Cassandra, a captive? There is a sexual element in this hatred also: it is as though Clytemnestra has manned herself in unmanning Agamemnon.

Her final outcry is made to Orestes, just before he takes her inside the house to kill her:

You are the snake I gave birth to, and gave the breast.

Her defiance and bitterness, her refusal of guilt or remorse, remains compellingly steadfast. ❀

Biography of
Aeschylus
(525 B.C. – 456 B.C.)

Though he remains undisputed as the first great playwright, not much is known of Aeschylus the man. Indeed, relatively little is known even of Aeschylus the playwright. Only seven of his estimated ninety plays are preserved in their entirety, and though he always wrote in trilogies, only one—the *Oresteia*—has survived intact.

Born of noble parents, Aeschylus probably lived at Eleusis, near Athens. He fought at Marathon in 490 (where he was wounded, and his brother killed), and again at Artemisium and Salamis in 480. Some of his military experiences were to find expression in *Persae,* the only surviving Greek tragedy to take for its subject recent events rather than myth.

Aeschylus was an early champion at the Great Dionysia, the dramatic competition in which a handful of playwrights annually vied for honors. His first known participation was in 499, his first win in 484; in all, he took the first prize thirteen times. (According to records, he lost to Sophocles in 468, but rallied in time for a victory the following year.) Aeschylus probably traveled at least twice to Syracuse, where his plays were produced at the court of Hieron I. He died at Gela on the south coast of Sicily, in 456, and was accorded full public honors.

Drama before Aeschylus had consisted of only a chorus and one actor. The actor could assume different parts by changing masks, but he was mostly limited to linear recitation—a bare step above the Homeric rhapsodes. By adding a second actor, Aeschylus expanded exponentially the possibilities for dialogue, transforming a genre that described action into one that depicted it—in effect, inventing tragedy. He is said to have taken an active hand in all aspects of performance, designing sets, training singers and dancers, and likely appearing in his own plays.

The Aeschylean theater feels less immediately modern than that of Euripides, and the grand scale of his designs can make them seem remote. Modern readers are accustomed to privileging character above other concerns, but as Brooks Otis notes of Agamemnon, "What matters is not what [he] does or suffers but what his action and suffering represent." Thus Clytemnestra, for instance, easily dominates the *Oresteia's* first play, of which she is the prime mover. But since it is her son Orestes who motivates the *Choephori*, Clytemnestra's importance (and her share of time onstage) there contracts to parallel that of the king in *Agamemnon*. Since Aeschylus' purpose was not character study, his plays tend to rely on types, subordinating personality to the broader goal of realizing a particular moral universe. Where he did write characters, however, his dramatic power can be overwhelming: Few dramatic roles rival the extraordinary richness and resonance of the *Agamemnon's* Clytemnestra.

Virginia Woolf famously remarked that Aeschylus liked to "stretch every phrase to the utmost," and he is as renowned for his metaphors as Homer is for his similes. One characteristic technique is to weave a single motif throughout a play—as with the lion cub in *Agamemnon,* or the ship of state in the *Hepta epi Theobas*—often describing it with the same phrases or words. Aeschylean tragedy is also marked by a love of spectacle. Though we can rely only on text, choreography and song were crucial to the total experience of Greek drama. (Among modern critics, H. D. F. Kitto has attempted to interpolate the role of the dance in the *Agamemnon,* and Oliver Taplin writes extensively on Aeschylean stagecraft.) An early *Life* of Aeschylus went so far as to claim that women in the audience had been known to miscarry, so intense were his dramatic effects. While apocryphal, the legend remains an object lesson in the shock value of Aeschylus' necessarily "experimental" theater. As an illustration, Taplin spotlights the terrifying impact made by the Furies, who twice assume the stage, not collectively as an ordered chorus, but singly and from all directions—a relentless swarm of individual avengers.

Much critical attention has been paid to the question of theodicy in Aeschylus. For generations, scholars warred incessantly over "the justice of Zeus," unintentionally blurring it with a monotheism imported from Judeo-Christian thought. The playwright undoubtedly had religious concerns; for instance, Jacqueline de Romilly suggests that his treatment of time flows directly out of his belief in divine justice. But it would be an error to think of Aeschylus as sermonizing. His Zeus does not arrive at decisions which he then enacts

in the mortal world; rather, human events are themselves an enactment of divine will. As Thomas Rosenmeyer has noted, "In
Aeschylus, as in Homer, the two levels of causation, the supernatural
and the human, are co-existent and simultaneous, two ways of
describing the same event." Thus, in one sense Agamemnon obviously does not want to kill his daughter. The decision made, however, *atē* necessarily strikes, and the king's nature alters as a matter of
course: "his spirit veering black, impure, unholy, / once he turned he
stopped at nothing." He is both agent and victim of circumstance; it
is not a case of either-or. Rosenmeyer cautions against the tendency
to impose our own framework upon the gods: "[T]he text defines
their being. For a critic to construct an Aeschylean theology would
be as quixotic as designing a typology of Aeschylean man. The needs
of the drama prevail."

Aeschylus is, unfortunately, extremely difficult to translate. Simon
Goldhill shows that the graded meanings of a single word (*dikē*) can
shift the meaning of an entire play. Likewise, N. G. L. Hammond has
demonstrated that the Greek *moira,* typically approximated as "fate,"
is better rendered as "apportionment"; and even this minor difference easily skews the depth of Agamemnon's guilt, or Orestes' innocence. (Less crucial, but still interesting connotations also are lost:
For instance, the word the Elders use to call Helen a woman "of
many men" is the same word used to describe a city as "populous"!)
For the Greekless reader, Robert Fagles' 1966 *Oresteia* is one of the
best modern translations of Aeschylus into English. ❧

Plot Summary of the
Agamemnon

Legend granted reunion and triumph to Odysseus, but prepared an unseemly end for Agamemnon. The death of the taker of Troy is called "sacrilegious" by the elders, an "outrage" by Cassandra; and themes of disorder, of misbegotten gain, and of the perversion of nature and right (*dikē*) are to saturate Aeschylus' play from its opening scene.

The Watchman, with whom the play begins, speaks for Argos as well as himself; both await a deliverance that will be no deliverance at all. His speech establishes two of the play's major inversions, between light/darkness and male/female. For the light from Troy is a false light, signaling not redemption but a new darkness. And almost the first thing we learn about the central woman of the plot is that she has the heart of a man.

The Chorus now provide a formal introduction to the events surrounding the play. Ten years ago, Menelaus, with Agamemnon, had led the fabled thousand ships to Troy to recover his bride Helen. The Chorus compare them to "vultures robbed of their young," in a simile which applies less to the erotically bereaved Menelaus than to Agamemnon's wife, Clytemnestra. Traditionally auspicious themes continue to show corrupt: The onset of battle is called by the name of the marriage-rite (*proteleia*), and fertility is drained for a wasteful war.

An omen had appeared to the Atreidae at Aulis, of twin eagles rending a pregnant hare. In this, Calchas revealed the anger of Artemis, who would stay the wind to Troy unless Agamemnon sacrificed his daughter, Iphigeneia. The seer also warned of the Fury that avenges children—a reference that hearkens forward to Clytemnestra but also back to Thyestes.

The Chorus now break their narrative to address the "Hymn to Zeus." Consensus has never been reached on its role in the play, but care should be taken not to assume later Western notions of an ennoblement unique to suffering (as suggested by Richmond Lattimore's "Wisdom comes alone through suffering"). As Peter Smith wryly noted, "Surely the striking thing about wisdom and suffering in the *Oresteia* is their separation."

The reasons for Artemis' wrath are not wholly clear. Does she loathe the eagles' feast itself, or what it represents—the death of a hare, or the coming devastation of Troy? The greater debate, however, has surrounded Agamemnon's culpability. We are meant to understand that the killing of a young maiden—essentially in exchange for the promiscuous Helen—is disproportionate; yet so is Clytemnestra's vengeance. Denys Page and Hugh Lloyd-Jones held that Agamemnon was the mere victim of an angry god. But a more probable reading allows for the intertwining of freedom and necessity in all moral choice. E. R. Dodds put it best by saying that Agamemnon *gave away* his freedom, "[slipping] his neck in the strap of Fate." The war is defended in the name of Zeus Xenios (god of hosts), but Zeus never required that offenses against hospitality be avenged at any cost: Agamemnon's determination was Agamemnon's choice. The description of Iphigenia's death, given now, is heart-rending; and her songs at the third libation are to be vividly recalled when Clytemnestra drives home her third blow explicitly as an offering to Zeus, lord of the dead.

Clytemnestra has been onstage throughout the parodos, an example of the Aeschylean "silent actor" lambasted by Aristophanes. The Chorus are skeptical of her abilities and judgment—she is, after all, a woman. But her formidable resource is quickly established in the extraordinary "beacon speech," a sweeping catalog of the installation of fire-signals by which news of victory is to be carried from Troy. Clytemnestra has engineered this: She has a will that does not bow to nature, and her very language is Olympian. (Even her lights are not mere lights, but proceed from Hephaestus—another irony, for to dream of Hephaestus was said to portend adultery.) Thomas Rosenmeyer notes, moreover, that since most of the speech's nouns are gendered, their jostling linguistically mirrors the play's sexual conflicts. A Herald confirms the end of the war, and Clytemnestra reproves her doubters, vaunting her eagerness to see "the people's darling"—the people's, not her own. She denies the rumors of adultery with Aegisthus: "in ill repute I am / as practiced as I am in dying bronze"—clearly looking forward to when she is indeed to dye bronze, drenching a sword with her husband's blood.

The Chorus now tell the parable of a lion cub, adopted and loved by its keepers, which only betrayed its true nature on reaching maturity: "the parent strain broke out / and it paid its breeders back." The cub refers primarily to Helen, but Bernard Knox has demonstrated that it represents as well Clytemnestra, Aegisthus, Orestes, and even Agamemnon. The lyric also continues to link fertility-rite and death ("she whirled her wedding to a stabbing end,"). These motifs—of evil that incubates, and sins that breed—are central to the *Oresteia*.

Agamemnon arrives, with his captive Cassandra, and is greeted by his wife with a fulsome speech of welcome. Some critics believe her tales of attempted suicide are true—that Electra's innocence at the opening of *Choephori* hints at an earlier, purer Clytemnestra. But she herself gives little sign of this. She invokes Calchas' imagery of the net that took Troy, saying that if her king had been wounded as often as she was told he would have been "gashed like a dragnet." Her language is magnificent, ceding nothing, and no less is her command to her serving-women: to line the king's way with costly carpets, that his feet might not touch the earth. There is an echo of *Odyssey* XXIII in Clytemnestra's comparison of her sight of Agamemnon to that of a shipwrecked sailor coming near to land—but it is precisely her difference from Penelope that rules the scene.

Agamemnon, who has doubtless heard of his wife's infidelity, comments wryly that her welcome, like his absence, has been too long. He initially refuses her invitation, but in a half-dozen lines she has beaten down every objection, deftly bending his answers to her will. Robert Goheen showed that Aeschylus intended the carpets to be not purple, but dark red. Agamemnon's progress into the palace thus supplies a visual metaphor for his crimes, a way that has left a trail of blood. His trampling of costly things further parallels the original crime of the adulterer Thyestes, who "[trampled] on his brother's bed."

Clytemnestra's speech, as Agamemnon enters the palace, claims dominion over the sea as her beacons had over the land, and reverberates throughout with a sense of endlessness ("There is the sea / and who shall drain it dry?" The queen's language, her ambition, her grief for Iphigeneia—all are bottomless.

The Chorus, now alone, express a foreboding they can ill understand. Clytemnestra unexpectedly reappears to summon Cassandra, but her invitations meet with an impenetrable silence: Cassandra is, indeed, the only figure in the play not to bow immediately before the queen's will. When Clytemnestra gives up in frustration, the Chorus' tentative overtures are abruptly cut by screams from the girl, who describes the cannibal feast of Thyestes in images cinematic in their immediacy and terror. Having violated a marriage-pact to Apollo, Cassandra can see both past and future, but is doomed never to be believed. She thus describes the impending murder—and stoically goes forward to meet her own doom—but meets only incomprehension all the while. The Chorus' ineffectualness is stressed for a purpose: Even when Agamemnon cries out, they assume the killer has come from outside, and are unable to act to save him.

The palace doors now open to reveal a grisly tableau: Agamemnon has been caught in robes and murdered in his bath. The intimacy of the killing is particularly chilling: It occurs in a ritual between husband and wife, perverted—like all sexuality in this play—and steeped in death. The actual slaying is described explicitly in the terms of a bull's ritual slaughter, and according to Walter Burkert, may have arisen from sacrificial ritual.

Clytemnestra, at last able to speak freely, gives vent to all the fury of her years of waiting: "Here I stand and here I struck / and here my work is done." The most horrifying moment comes when she revels in the splash of her husband's blood:

> [Clytemnestra has] cast Agamemnon in the role of Heaven and herself in the role of Earth, while the spurt of blood stood for the gentle falling of the rain/semen; she transformed the ancient world's supreme symbol of love between the sexes into her own supreme symbol of hatred. In the moment of murdering her husband, she intuited something more terrifying even than murder: a universe divided by open war between the male and the female . . .
> (John Herington)

Clytemnestra takes special "relish" in the slaying of her husband's mistress. Her work, she says, is just (*dikē*), and to the Chorus' outrage she at once returns indignation, asking why there were no recriminations when Iphigeneia was killed. Gradually, however, she shifts her defense and claims that she acted as the retributive spirit of Thyestes—that she was herself the Fury of the house. She hauntingly visualizes Iphigeneia, on the banks of the Styx, welcoming her father and murderer to death. The Chorus are reluctantly persuaded that

Clytemnestra may have been justified, and warn again of crimes to come. But the queen, audacious as ever, believes the cycle can be broken and that she will break it.

Only now does Aegisthus arrive with his bodyguard. He immediately proves sniveling and ineffectual—the "wolf" to Clytemnestra's "lioness"—and is derided by the Chorus for letting a woman do the man's work of revenge. Insults are exchanged to the point of drawn swords, but Clytemnestra calmly stays the conflict. The play closes with her renewed vow to "set the house in order once for all" — though whether this can be achieved by human means, remains to be seen. ✿

List of Characters in the
Agamemnon

The play opens on Clytemnestra's **Watchman,** who has kept a year-long vigil for the beacon-light from Troy. Aeschylus ironically has him hail the "dawn of the darkness" and identify his own fortune with Agamemnon's, not realizing that the truth of both events is directly the opposite of his expectations.

Queen of Argos, and half-sister to Helen of Troy, **Clytemnestra** towers over and essentially directs the events of the *Agamemnon.* Though stress is laid on her "maleness of heart," her femininity runs implicitly through her account of the war, which focuses on bereavement rather than on honor or glory. R. P. Winnington-Ingram has suggested that Clytemnestra's resentment of Agamemnon derives not only from his murder of their daughter, but also from his status as a man.

Despite the assurance of Clytemnestra's beacons, the Chorus refuse to believe that the war has ended until a **Herald** arrives from Troy. He describes the ruin of the Greek ships, in a storm that seemed auspiciously to spare Agamemnon's fleet, but in fact only saved him for a worse fate. The Herald also reports that Menelaus is missing, but presumed alive (Menelaus probably featured in the lost satyr-play to the *Oresteia,* the *Proteus*).

Though he led the troops at Troy, and was responsible for the death of Iphigeneia, **Agamemnon**'s own personality makes little or no impression. As Thomas Rosenmeyer puts it, "It is not that Agamemnon is a flat character [but] that he is merely a type." His wrongful estimate of Odysseus (whom he names as a man particularly worthy of trust!) prepares us for his fatal misjudgment of his wife, Clytemnestra.

Agamemnon took **Cassandra** as his concubine at Troy. Despite her prophetic powers, she is fated never to be believed, and the Chorus fail to understand her warnings until it is too late. Her part is almost wholly concerned with revenges, weaving present acts into a cosmology of crimes and punishments. In describing Agamemnon's murder moments before it occurs, Cassandra also "unfocuses [it] in time" (John Herington), lending the play a sheen of surreality.

Though Clytemnestra claims to rely on his strength for protection, **Aegisthus** quickly shows himself to be the smallest figure in the play. Lacking courage or conviction, he is swaggeringly anxious to defend his rights, yet fails to intimidate even the Argive elders. Thomas Rosenmeyer has aptly described him as "a character by subtraction."

Too old to fight at Troy, the **Chorus** of Argive elders have remained helpless witnesses to the decline of the house. They characteristically understand less of what is happening than we do, failing utterly to grasp Cassandra's warnings and able to muster only impotent threats against the murderers of their king. ✾

Critical Views on
Agamemnon

H. D. F. KITTO ON THEATER AND DANCE

[H. D. F. Kitto was Chair of Greek in the Department of Classics and Ancient History at the University of Bristol. His works include *Greek Tragedy: A Literary Study* (1939), *Form and Meaning in Drama: A Study of Six Greek Plays and of* Hamlet (1956), and *Poiesis: Structure and Thought* (1966). In this extract, he reminds us that the text of an Aeschylean drama shows us only one part of its total theatrical effect.]

⟨. . .⟩ The first ode, the *parodos,* falls into three clearly marked sections. To begin with, there are three stanzas mainly in dactyls, which deal with the omen. Then comes what we may call the Hymn to Zeus, and that is in trochees. The third section deals with Agamemnon's sacrificing of Iphigeneia, and is composed in the iambic rhythm, though with dramatic excursions into other metres. ⟨. . .⟩ In the second ode there are seven stanzas; with the exception of the song-like refrain appended to each of the first six, the iambic rhythm prevails throughout. The third ode contains eight stanzas. The first pair are in trochees and anacreontics, the second pair in glyconics. With the third pair the iambics return, giving place to more anacreontics, but the fourth pair is entirely iambic. The fourth ode, we observe, does not use the iambic rhythm at all, but it comes back later, with the responding passages. In other words, ⟨. . .⟩ seventeen out of twenty-one consecutive stanzas are composed, either wholly or in part, in this one rhythm. Aeschylus has done something quite unusual, but it is easy to see why he did it. ⟨. . .⟩

In the first ode this rhythm presents to us the following ideas: the adverse winds, Agamemnon's hard choice, the mad frenzy ⟨. . .⟩ which swept him over the brink, the killing of Iphigeneia, and the foreboding of the chorus that some evil must come of it. Now, it is surely a necessary conclusion that the sustaining of this rhythm implies that a corresponding dance-movement also was sustained, and presumably music of a certain mode too. When the second ode begins, in the same rhythm, we can safely assume that the same general dance-movement and music began with it. But the second ode begins with Paris. ⟨. . .⟩

⟨T⟩he little which we can discern of the dance can be an extra control over dramatic interpretation. It has been said of this ode that the chorus begins in a mood of joy and relief at the victory, but then, as it considers what the victory has cost, changes to a mood of apprehension. This may sound plausible, but the rhythm disproves it; Aeschylus knew enough about music and dancing to realise that joy and fear call for different rhythms; but here he uses the same one throughout. What the chorus says about Paris cannot be an expression of joy; the ode begins with a dance-movement which is now firmly associated in our minds with the crime of Agamemnon, the frenzy that possessed him, and the threat of evil to come. Therefore, when the second ode begins ⟨. . .⟩, the dance of itself would link Paris with Agamemnon. He is not an enemy in whose destruction the chorus is exulting; he is, like Agamemnon, one whom temptation has swept over the brink ⟨. . .⟩. But Paris is already destroyed; the parallel is no encouraging one. Then, for the rest of the ode, we continue to watch this same dance, whatever it is; and as we do so, we hear of Helen's sin, how it brought sorrow and death to Greece. Still the dance continues: ashes came back in the place of living men, there is anger against the Atreidae, the gods do not disregard men of blood.

So far, then, we can say that the dance put immediately and vividly before the very eyes of the audience an idea which we, reading the text, can miss entirely. The destruction of Paris is yet another reason to be fearful about Agamemnon.

The third ode begins with totally different dance-movements, ⟨. . .⟩: Helen was welcomed with songs at Troy, but the songs turned to dirges. Then comes the simple parable of the lion's cub, in glyconics. ⟨. . .⟩

⟨. . .⟩ It is back again, that iambic rhythm, now charged with the ideas of sin and its inevitable consequence, ruin. It swerves aside, ⟨. . .⟩ for a moment into anacreontics; but it comes back for the final two stanzas, which give us explicitly the doctrine of hybris and ate. Then, as this obstinate rhythm at last subsides, Agamemnon enters the theatre, royally, with Cassandra. This is the magnificent climax to which it has all been leading. It does not seem too much to say, that in all this even we, peering through a glass darkly, can see how Aeschylus gave visible shape, in the orchestra, to the conception that sin leads to more sin, and that to disaster. ⟨. . .⟩

—H. D. F. Kitto, "The Dance in Greek Tragedy," *Journal of Hellenic Studies* 75 (1955): pp. 36–37.

Robert F. Goheen on Blood and Light

[Robert F. Goheen served as president of Princeton University and was later appointed Ambassador to India. He is the author of *The Imagery of Sophocles'* Antigone: *A Study of Poetic Language and Structure* (1951) and *The Human Nature of a University* (1969). In this essay, he suggests a thematic link between the carpets spread by Clytemnestra (in the first play) and the festal robes of the newly-reconciled Erinyes (in the third).]

⟨T⟩he colors of blood and death lurk in the carpet and have significance there. Verbal imagery of *blood on the ground* forms a recurring motif, carefully articulated and impressively sustained. Significantly it gets its first explicit statement in the choral ode which immediately follows the carpet-scene, and from here it is carried through the trilogy to form one of the more patent lines which bind the three plays into a single whole. In the ode following the carpet-scene, the figure of a man's dark, death-marking blood on the ground is part of the agitation and fear that weigh hard upon the Chorus. Blood once shed, they see, is beyond all recall ⟨...⟩.

⟨The image⟩ reads from this point on through the entire *Oresteia*. In the *Choephori* it appears three times; and in the most fully delineated of these the figure is adapted to crystallize the vengeful ethos of that play. ⟨...⟩ Blood-vengeance in this play lays claim to being a "Law" set in the ultimate nature of things; here it is part of the vitalism of blood itself and is inexorable. In the *Eumenides,* however, the earlier and countering sensitivity reemerges in terms of blood on the ground. That is to say, both of the previous general applications of the image are caught up and repeated in the third play: the irremediable finality of death and blood's demand for blood. ⟨...⟩

⟨I⟩t is a major function of the concluding portion of the third play to convert the forces and images of blood, blight, and destruction into forces and images of physical and moral fecundity in the life of the city; a striking development at the very close is a red-robed, torch procession, the color (*phoinix*) of whose robes relates closely to the color *porphyreos* and, metaphorically, transmutes the earlier threat of serried bloodshed into a recognized and respected prophylactic symbol. ⟨...⟩

Thus the final spectacle of the *Eumenides* offers us, in company with the red robes, a chanting, torch-bearing, ritual procession. The procession moves off in an aura of solemn but expansive benevolence, raising as its refrain the *ololugmos* cry of victory. In the *Agamemnon* the light bearing and ritual chant of this procession have had specific prototypes whose promise has been blasted, their effect turned to the negative. For the ending of the long destructive war torches were carried around to altars and the *ololugmos* was raised. ⟨. . .⟩ Moreover, the light in word and torch which helps close the *Eumenides* had its spectacular first blaze in the beacon of the *Agamemnon*. The imagery of light, with its traditional connotations of liberation and of hope, is forcefully initiated there, carried verbally through the *Choephori*, and brought to its final positive turn at the close of the *Eumenides*. In the first play these elements (the beacon, the lighting of the altars with torch procession, the *ololugmos*) have expressed a joy in victory and prospect of liberation from long sorrow only to have that joy turn to fresh sorrow and to have us discover that the expression has been engineered as a masking prelude for an act of planned destructiveness. In the last play these same elements are reintroduced to culminate the reverse movement from destructiveness to safety, from anguish to hope. The connections and development are clear, and the guidance they afford seems surely to indicate a planned connection from strikingly colored carpet to strikingly colored robes. If the carpet was, as we have been led to feel, an ominous blood color, then the "red" of the robes is its inverted restatement. It represents the conversion of the (darkly) lethal carpet into a (perhaps more brightly tinted) symbol of blessing. Blood has been taken up off the ground and made an element in the sacramental life of the city.

—Robert F. Goheen, "Aspects of Dramatic Symbolism: Three Studies in the *Oresteia*," *American Journal of Philology* 7, no. 2 (1955): pp. 118, 119–20, 122–23, 124.

FROMA ZEITLIN ON IPHIGENIA AND THE IMAGERY OF SACRIFICE

[Froma Zeitlin is Chair of the Classics Department at Princeton University, and author of *Under the Sign of the Shield: Semiotics and Aeschylus'* Seven Against Thebes (1982) and *Playing the Other: Gender and Society in Classical Greek Literature* (1995). Here, she shows how the language of ritual slaughter is applied to all seven of the killings described in the *Agamemnon:* "[T]he sacrifice of Iphigenia becomes the symbol which the other murders resemble as unlawful deeds."]

⟨. . .⟩ *Proteleia* is a ritual word signifying preliminary sacrifices of any kind, but especially those performed before the marriage ceremony. A favorable and auspicious term of sacrifice, then, is used in an image of men slain in the battles preliminary to the final destruction of Troy. ⟨. . .⟩ ⟨The⟩ coming death of *Agamemnon* is darkly riddled ⟨. . .⟩. *Teleitai,* that word of many meanings, primarily connotes fulfillment or end. However, in its punning word play with *proteleia,* it assumes the color of its kindred definition, the performance of a holy rite. ⟨. . .⟩

⟨. . .⟩ ⟨T⟩he chorus returns again to its reminiscences of the world of the past and recalls another sacrifice, which is the second act of violence described, the feasting of the eagles upon the hare. As a portent, the act itself is a symbol, susceptible of broad interpretation ⟨. . .⟩. We note here only that the initial verb of feasting, *boskomenoi* and the characterization of the perpetrators as *lagodaitas* give way to the typical verb of sacrifice *thyō* ⟨. . .⟩.

⟨Agamemnon sacrifices⟩ his daughter as *proteleia naōn.* In this context, *proteleia* is used with greater effect than before. Iphigenia was literally the preliminary sacrifice before the departure of the fleet, but we are reminded too that she was a nubile young girl (*parthenosphagoisin, partheniou haimatos, ataurōtos,* and that, according to the tradition, she was lured to Aulis with the promise of marriage to Achilles. Instead of offering *proteleia,* she herself became the *proteleia.* ⟨. . .⟩

The fourth specific deed of bloodshed appears in the parable of the lion cub ⟨. . .⟩. The cub is characterized as *hiereus tis Atas.* The *hiereus* is not simply a priest but the priest who presides at sacrifices, technically a *sphageus*. ⟨...⟩

⟨...⟩ That ⟨Cassandra⟩ regards these crimes in terms of ritual is evident from her description of the house to which she has been brought ⟨...⟩. *Androsphageion* is translated as a slaughter place for men, *pedorrhantērion* as a floor dripping with blood. Fraenkel comments that the "awful word *pedorrhantērion* must have evoked in the mind of the audience the name of a sacral vessel, the *perirrhantērion,* an instrument of ritual purification, whereas here the most monstrous defilement is meant." Similarly the term *androsphageion* includes not only the concept of *sphagē*, a term used in sacrifice, but also recalls the *sphageion,* a ritual vessel for catching the blood of the sacrifice. ⟨...⟩

⟨...⟩ Agamemnon's blood is a libation, and with the three strokes ⟨Clytemnestra⟩ gave him, each one drenching her in blood, she makes precise allusion to the customary rite of pouring three libations after the feast—one to the Olympians, one to the Chthonians, and one to Zeus the Savior. ⟨...⟩

Aeschylus ⟨...⟩ unifies the murders by revealing their relationship to the sacrifice of Iphigenia as effects of the same cause—the curse on the house—and he further unifies them as all partaking of the peculiar horror and lawlessness of her death. It is curious to note that the actual moment of Iphigenia's sacrifice is never described. The chorus tells us in heartbreaking detail of the preparations for her immolation, but at the instant the knife is poised above the throat, a great ox sits upon their tongue ⟨...⟩. They need say no more. The sacrificial descriptions of the other murders plainly tell us how Iphigenia must have met her end. The device of this imagery, then, illuminates the common nature of the murders. ⟨...⟩

—Froma Zeitlin, "The Motif of the Corrupted Sacrifice in Aeschylus' *Oresteia," Transactions and Proceedings of the American Philological Association* 96 (1965): pp. 465–68, 473, 489.

JACQUELINE DE ROMILLY ON CASSANDRA AND AESCHYLEAN TIME

[Jacqueline de Romilly is Professor Emeritus of Greek Literature at the Sorbonne and a member of the Académie Française. English translations of her work include *Thucydides and Athenian Imperialism* (1963), *Magic and Rhetoric in Ancient Greece* (1975), and *The Great Sophists in Periclean Athens* (1992). Less than one-fifth of the *Agamemnon* occurs in the present; here, de Romilly explains how Agamemnon's manipulation of time relates to his belief in divine—albeit delayed—justice.]

⟨. . .⟩ The result is, of course, a perpetual oscillation in these plays between past and present. But this oscillation is not just haphazard and disorderly. Indeed, if we look a little more closely into the structure of the different plays, it emerges that, quite often, Aeschylus keeps for the center of his play the most distant "flashback," as we should say now, and joins it there with an anticipation and prediction about future events. So that the whole sequence of events stands there in the middle, as one great unity, where time's continuous course is gathered into a legible pattern. ⟨. . .⟩

⟨T⟩wo opposite events have to be explained: Agamemnon's victory over Troy, and Agamemnon's murder—that is to say, we must hear of two different kinds of crimes. ⟨. . .⟩

The result is that the play is long (it has almost 1,700 lines), but has no more than about 300 lines dealing with the present time. All the rest of the play describes the past—whether narrations of the war (as in the scene with the messenger) or memories of previous events (as in most chorus-songs).

In fact, it can be said that all chorus-songs, till the murder of Agamemnon, deal with the past. ⟨. . .⟩

⟨B⟩efore Agamemnon's doom comes his success. And this success has its causes in another fault, in somebody else's fault—namely Paris' fault and the rape of Helen. That is why the two following songs of the chorus deal with this more distant crime. The first is devoted to Paris, the second to Helen. ⟨. . .⟩ Now this, of course, explains the Trojan disaster; but, by a remarkable twist of composition, Aeschylus has succeeded in making these two songs, and particularly the first one, begin with Paris' fault but end with Agamemnon's. Paris' fault has brought the war; the war and its miseries are Agamemnon's doing: he ordained this war, where so many men died "for another man's wife," and "resentful grief grows against the Atridae, principals in this suit." We have, at the same time, a more distant flashback than before, showing the Trojan fault, and a new fault for Agamemnon, making his case still worse.

But then, one could object, is there no flashback into a more distant past? Is there no mention of Atreus' crime of obliging his brother Thyestes to eat his own children? Of course there is. We should expect it to be right in the middle of the play, just before Agamemnon's death; and there it is. Only these distant crimes are not mentioned in a chorus-song, but in Cassandra's scene. As in the *Persians* and in the *Prometheus,* we have a real prophet—one who is entitled to explain both the past and the future. More: we have here a prophet with visions, who actually sees, all at the same time, all together, in one single perception, the whole time fused into one. ⟨. . .⟩ Aeschylus could not find a more powerful or startling way to suggest that these crimes were but one with Atreus' crime. ⟨. . .⟩ Atreus, Agamemnon, Orestes: the three generations suddenly stand before our eyes as one. ⟨. . .⟩

⟨. . .⟩ Nor do the mentions of the past stop there. Only, after the murder, we find them no longer in the chorus-songs, but in the murderer's explanations.

The sacrifice of Iphigeneia and the daimon attached to the house are Clytemnestra's excuses. They come first, and the murder of Iphigeneia is mentioned several times. Atreus' crime, on the other hand, is Aegisthus' excuse; for he is Thyestes' son. And, just as in the first part of the play, this most distant flashback comes in last. The whole range of causes, which were developed at length in the first part of the play, where they gave birth to fear, is here taken again and repeated, in a shorter manner, so as to provide arguments. This means we actually see in the *Agamemnon* divine justice announcing human justice and making a place for it, just as we see the search for the causes of punishment leading the way toward the judiciary discussion about the legitimacy of punishment. In that respect, the *Agamemnon* prepares for the *Eumenides,* and further on for the plays of Euripides, with past actions discussed in parallel debates.

—Jacqueline de Romilly, *Time in Greek Tragedy* (Ithaca: Cornell University Press, 1968): pp. 72–73, 77–81.

[John J. Peradotto is Andrew V. V. Raymond Professor of Classics at the State University of New York at Buffalo. He is the author of *Man in the Middle Voice: Name and Narration in the* Odyssey (1990), and a former editor of *Arethusa*. This extract shows how the innovation of the eagle-omen emphasizes Agamemnon's role as destroyer of the innocent over his role as enemy of Troy (with whom Artemis sided in the *Iliad*). Aeschylus' Agamemnon cannot be perceived as merely the god's passive victim; rather, his choice and tragedy are a re-enactment of the Heraclitean edict, "Character is fate."]

The omen of the eagles and the hare bears no significant correspondence to anything in the poetic tradition about the *second* gathering at Aulis. But it does closely resemble the omen observed at the *first* gathering forecasting an Argive victory in the tenth year: a snake devouring a sparrow and her eight nestlings. Aeschylus has seen fit to conflate the two gatherings at Aulis into one in such a way that the omen of the eagles and the hare does double service as prediction of an Argive victory and as emblem of Artemis' wrath. Still, it remains to ask why the poet should not be satisfied merely to reproduce the omen of the snake and sparrows so well-known from the *Iliad*. ⟨. . .⟩

An introductory clue to our question is the statement of a scholiast on Aristophanes' Lysist. 645. ⟨. . .⟩ ⟨with the idea of Brauron and not Avlis as the site of Agamemnon's sacrifice of Iphigeneia⟩. ⟨D⟩uring Aeschylus' day, young Athenian girls, aged five through ten, customarily participated in the festival of Brauronian Artemis ⟨. . .⟩. During excavations at Brauron begun in 1948, under the direction of John Papadimitriou, votive statuettes wre unearthed representing a young girl ⟨. . .⟩ holding a hare. ⟨. . .⟩

> Artemis Brauronia . . . was associated with Iphigeneia and adored as Protectress of birth and fertility—especially animal fertility. But we are able to say now that the name of Iphegeneia is one of the *hypostases* of the great chthonian goddess—the Earth-mother—and the cult remained continually associated with the same site even after the abandonment of the prehistoric town. It was much later that the goddess became confused with Artemis and the name became an epithet of Artemis. . . . We must

⟨T⟩he Artemis at Brauron is a goddess whose main concerns are
fertility, pregnancy, youth, innocence, but around whose cult there
are whispers of human sacrifice. The Artemis of the *Agamemnon* is
no other; the devouring of a pregnant hare and her brood dramatizes one aspect of her Brauronian character, while the sacrifice of
Iphigeneia dramatizes the other. Such a goddess would indeed resent
the murder of Thyestes' children, the murder of Iphigeneia, and the
murder of innocent youth at Troy. ⟨T⟩he omen subsumes all three
events, relating them one to another as cases of the slaughter of
innocent youth in the pursuit and exercise of power.

The text supports this triple reference. Treating the hare's death as
a *sacrifice* and a *meal,* underscores its relationship with the sacrificial
feast of Thyestes' children, and to the sacrificial death of Iphigeneia,
which, though it is not a meal, does not get by without some allusion to eating. But treated as a *hunt,* the omen clearly refers to Troy
and its inhabitants. ⟨. . .⟩

⟨T⟩he capture of Troy is described as the casting of a hunting-net
from which neither old nor young can extricate themselves. ⟨. . .⟩

⟨. . .⟩ If, as is unlikely, the terms of the omen itself were not sufficient to have reminded a fifth-century audience of the Homeric
Agamemnon's desire, memorable in its ferocity, that every Trojan
perish utterly, *including the unborn child in the womb,* then this passage would surely have done so ⟨. . .⟩. ⟨T⟩he Argives, especially their
commander, are not mere hunters, but vicious, pitiless, indiscrimi-
nate hunters, who must naturally incur the hatred of her in whose
honour young hares, as Xenophon tells us, were traditionally spared
by huntsmen. ⟨. . .⟩

⟨. . .⟩ Agamemnon is *free* to sacrifice or not to sacrifice Iphigeneia,
to pursue the war against Troy or not to do so. ⟨. . .⟩

The statement "Zeus sent the Atreidae . . ." is a religious interpretation of the chorus, not an empirical description. ⟨. . .⟩ Zeus Xenios
permits, justifies, supports the war, but nothing in the text suggests
that he *obliges.* ⟨. . .⟩

⟨O⟩nly for the king himself is the disproportion in his vengeance a point of pride. ⟨. . .⟩

A young girl's innocent blood is shed to launch a war for an adulterous woman, involving a holocaust of victims and regicide. The war is thus a demonic perversion of society's extermination of the offender recognized as a public menace. The moral condemnation implied in all these contrasts far outweighs the cold comfort that its legal sanction is the law of hospitality.

In his decision to sacrifice Iphigeneia and pursue the war for Helen Agamemnon suffers no external coercion. As we have tried to demonstrate, his choice depends less upon Zeus or Artemis than upon the kind of man he is, his ⟨*ethos*⟩. ⟨. . .⟩

⟨. . .⟩ Agamemnon's decision cannot be viewed as anything other than what the chorus calls it—a madness which cannot adjust personal desire and legal claim to the demands of a larger reality, and dares all in the face of doom. If Agamemnon is victimized, it is by his own ⟨*ethos*⟩ ⟨. . .⟩.

—John J. Peradotto, "The Omen of the Eagles and the Hare of Agamemnon," *Phoenix* 23, no. 3 (1969): pp. 243–48, 250–51, 255–57.

P. E. Easterling on Agamemnon's Surrender

[P. E. Easterling is Professor of Classics at Newnham College, Cambridge. She is the editor of *The Cambridge Companion to Greek Tragedy* (1997), and author of a commentary on Sophocles' *Trachiniae* (1982). Below, she considers the credibility and dramatic uses of Agamemnon's treading of the carpets.]

Should we be surprised after this onslaught if Agamemnon gives in? Yes, if we suppose that people are always rationally in control of themselves. ⟨. . .⟩

⟨S⟩urely the scene makes sense on the human level: a man succumbing to temptation and saying as he does so, 'I know this is wrong . . .' — *video meliora proboque, deteriora sequor*. It is humanly intelligible provided we can assume that walking on purple is something Agamemnon, or any successful Greek, might be expected to find attractive in itself, so long as he could be sure it was not dangerous. This is the essential point, as I see it, for our understanding of the scene; walking on purple is just not a feature of modern life, but if it can be thought of as something highly flattering to one's self-esteem, tangible proof that one has 'made it to the top', then we can understand the sequence of Agamemnon's confusion and collapse, his succumbing against his better judgement, under pressure from a woman assuring him that it is all perfectly safe, daring him, almost, to accept her challenge. ⟨. . .⟩

⟨His⟩ removal of his shoes when he decides to walk on the purple ⟨. . .⟩ is a gesture of respect for the precious material, and more important, a sign of god-fearing. ⟨. . .⟩ It contributes a visual detail which illustrates his knowledge that he is doing the wrong thing, and of course in human terms it is perfectly comprehensible: it represents the futile attempts we make to deceive and comfort ourselves when we know we have taken the wrong decision. ⟨. . .⟩

⟨I⟩n order to enter fully into this scene we have no need of the idea 'Agamemnon is a proud man' or 'Agamemnon is exhausted by all those years of warfare' or even 'he thinks she loves him, and he yields'. ⟨. . .⟩ I lay so much stress on believing in the characters and their actions because although great dramatists are often ambiguous they are not puzzling. To be puzzling is to run the risk of distracting or boring the audience; and every great dramatist knows that they must be gripped. So human behaviour is portrayed—through whatever artificial conventions or whatever fantasy—as something we can understand and identify with.

What is the carpet scene for? It cannot be thought of as having any practical effect on the action: however Agamemnon walks into the house, Clytemnestra can still attack him in the bath. Nor should it be given significance as the clinching act of *hubris* without which Agamemnon's death would not be inevitable. ⟨. . .⟩

The scene, then, must be considered to have a symbolic function ⟨. . .⟩. It shows how Agamemnon's deeds and their consequences are organically linked. ⟨. . .⟩

⟨It⟩ brings upon the stage an Agamemnon whose blindness recalls the Chorus's description of his behaviour at Aulis: 'When the wind of his purpose had veered about and blew impious, impure, unholy, from that moment he reversed his mind and turned to utter reck-lessness. For men are emboldened by base-counselling wretched infatuation, the beginning of woe'. And we recall Aulis, too, in the detail about the religious expert giving advice, which Agamemnon brings into the stichomythia. These echoes remind us of the load of guilt that Agamemnon still carries, and of the inescapability of his having to pay for it. The scene also looks forward. ⟨. . .⟩ ⟨I⟩t makes vivid the idea of punishment coming to Agamemnon; even more, by showing his blindness it convinces us that he is walking into a trap of which he has no suspicion.

⟨. . .⟩ The compulsions under which men act were given an external, supernatural character by Aeschylus and his contempo-raries, who interpreted human experience as part of a larger con-tinuum, the total working of the universe. Modern writers tend to look inwards, rather than outwards to the cosmic patterns, but the human raw material remains the same. The curse is not a remote and peculiar phenomenon, untranslatable into universal experience: we are *all* under a curse in the sense that we are caught in the web of necessity. As human beings we are forced to make choices and commit ourselves, and then to take the consequences for actions over which we are not fully in control, and our sufferings are often out of all proportion to our deserts.

—P. E. Easterling, "Presentation of Character in Aeschylus," Greece & Rome 20, no. 1 (1973): pp. 14–15, 17–19.

JOHN GOULD ON CHARACTER IN AESCHYLUS

[John Gould held the Henry Overton Wills Chair of Greek at the University of Bristol, and is author of *The Develop-ment of Plato's Ethics* (1955) and *Herodotus* (1989). Below, he explains how Aeschylus embeds his major personalities in the world of their plays.]

⟨. . .⟩ The answer lies, I think, in the public nature of Klytaimestra's language and the formal modes of speech which are the medium in which her personality exists. In these, and in the pervasive metaphorical colouring of the whole language of the play which ensures that we cannot quite detach Klytaimestra from what I have called the play's 'world'. ⟨. . .⟩

⟨H⟩er first two *rheseis* (the Beacon speech and the account of captured Troy) combine the 'objectivity' which we have already encountered as a mark of the trimeter speech with a sense of uncanny power, which is implicit in Klytaimestra's knowing, as though an eye-witness, of things distant and beyond her vision. It is almost as though she commands these things, but neither speech presents her in terms which we could construe as the workings of her own consciousness. Later, in the speeches to the Herald and to her husband, the same sense of awesome power is embodied in the ease with which they challenge and outface truth in the face of those who are witnesses to it and, through their staging, in what they convey of Klytaimestra's dominance of the house and of its threshold. Even the great speech after Agamemnon's murder is not so much a revelation of character, or even, quite, of personality in its ordinary, human dimensions, as a kind of demonic apparition, personality translated into terms of 'otherness': starting from the coolest and most collected of genitive absolutes, it displays not so much Klytaimestra as the power that haunts the play and prepares us for Klytaimestra's momentary vision of herself as the *alastor* of 'Atreus the feaster'. And, as I have suggested, these aspects of 'Klytaimestra' are diffused through the play and through the figures that inhabit it. Her sensuality reappears in the visual sharpness, the physical, sensual *presence,* in the Kassandra scene, of horrors past and horrors yet to be enacted (the house 'breathes' the scent of blood as she approaches it, and her uncanny power is reflected back at us in the equally uncanny, as I would argue, powerlessness of Agamemnon. ⟨. . .⟩

⟨W⟩hen Mrs. Easterling gives us instances of what is humanly intelligible within the dramatic frame, they are such things as 'it is easy enough to imagine a highly successful person in his moment of triumph being simplistic in this sort of way' or 'the scene makes sense on the human level. ⟨. . .⟩ I take Agamemnon's acts and words to *be* humanly intelligible, I take him to engage to the full not just our aesthetic attention but our moral attention also; to be, in fact, a fully realised paradigm of the human condition—or rather, to be part of such a paradigm. But this, as I see it, is where the ways divide. Because I take the paradigmatic force of *Agamemnon* to consist, not of a number of human figures behaving in ways in which, from my experience of myself or of others, I can imagine human figures separately behaving, but in the total image of human existence that the play presents. The play as a whole that is, is the 'meaning' that is to be humanly intelligible, the play as a whole being an image, a metaphor of the way things are, within human experience—not a literal enactment of 'the way people behave'. ⟨...⟩

—John Gould, "Dramatic Character and 'Human Intelligibility' in Greek Tragedy," *Proceedings of the Cambridge Philological Society* 204 (1978): pp. 59–62.

AYA BETENSKY ON CLYTEMNESTRA'S LANGUAGE

[Aya Betensky taught at Cornell University. In this essay, she examines Clytemnestra's motivations and psychology as revealed through her use of metaphor.]

⟨...⟩ In her eyes, her power is based on the connections she makes between herself, her own sexuality, and the elements of the natural world. ⟨...⟩ She thinks she can reverse nature by her actions and so reverse the cycle of crime breeding crime. ⟨...⟩

Clytemnestra's verbal accompaniment to Agamemnon's progress along the blood-red tapestries ⟨...⟩ extends her control of nature's resources in two directions. First, she has widened her sphere of control over fire and earth to include the element of water, the sea. The springs of her tears were drained long ago, but the resources of the sea are inexhaustible, and she is using them as lavishly and describing them as majestically as she did her tears and the beacon fires. She treats the sea as no more foreign or ungovernable than her own house. ⟨...⟩

Second, more clearly than before she is using nature in a way that is contrary to nature. The organic image of the vine is a logical continuation of her metaphors of protection and relief. The image is evocative and difficult to reduce to logic. The root suggests the dynasty of Agamemnon; its existence is a good thing because it protects the house. ⟨. . .⟩ The next two lines apply this statement (root/leaves provide shade) to Agamemnon, with an understandable reversal to warmth: it is characteristic of leaves to provide shade, of a man to keep his hearth warm in winter. The third statement in this series, however, does not simply reverse again to coolness, nor does it apply co-ordinately with the previous one to Agamemnon. *Thalpos men* connects with *hotan de . . . Zeus,* and the *de* clause raises the action to the divine level. Zeus is in control of vintage and seasons. Agamemnon is not the subject. The subject of the 'then' clause is *psuchos,* coolness, refreshing for Clytemnestra and her house, but chilling for others. Clytemnestra reinforces this change in emphasis by immediately addressing Zeus *teleios* with prayers for fulfilment. The vine is Agamemnon, the wine is his blood, and his home-coming will provide coolness and relief because it will also be his death. When blood is analogous to the sea's dye and to wine, nature is perverted. With enormous boldness she is ready to twist nature's creative fertility to her goal of destruction. ⟨. . .⟩ The sea's dye, the grape's wine, his blood, all will be drained to replace her tears and Iphigeneia's shed blood. ⟨. . .⟩

⟨Clytemnestra's⟩ description of her joy at Agamemnon's blood is the most shocking and memorable of all her lines in its twisting of ritual and creative natural process.

Even before she begins the formal comparison she reverses the terms, calling Agamemnon's blood, unexpectedly, a rain of dew. Her rejoicing is made the more shocking by being likened to the natural rejoicing of fields at rainfall, which comes from Zeus and is now termed neither rain nor dew but *ganos,* a bright liquid gladness. When she speaks of the libations she would like to make over the corpse, she equates *ganos* with blood and wine; and the sexual sense of *ganos* as semen is suggested by the 'birthpangs' of the bud, which conflate insemination, conception, and birthgiving. Again the same equation: again she is replenishing those dried-up springs of tears, as she anticipated in the image of the traveler and the spring, and the dye, and Iphigeneia's blood, with Agamemnon's. Now she thinks her fertility is restored.

The juxtaposition of creative fertility and her joy in destruction is jarring. But for her there is no discrepancy. Rather, the reversal is a righting of previous wrongs. ⟨. . .⟩

> —Aya Betensky, "Aeschylus' Oresteia: The Power of Clytemnestra," *Ramus* 7, no. 1 (1978): pp. 13, 18–20.

⟨🕮⟩

BROOKS OTIS ON STRUCTURE AND AGENCY

[Brooks Otis was Paddison Professor of Latin at the University of North Carolina at Chapel Hill. His books include *Virgil: A Study in Civilized Poetry* (1963) and *Ovid As an Epic Poet* (1966). In this extract, he shows how the relative importance of Aeschylean characters—and their relative placement in lyric (choruses, *commoi*) or trimeter (episodes)—hinges on their capacity to shift the terms of the play: "The difference... between Aeschylus and either Sophocles or Euripides is basically one of time, of the relation [of] two cosmic-historical *status quos,* one in which everything is shrouded in obscurity and beset by implicit contradictions and one in which everything is clarified or begins to be clarified."]

⟨. . .⟩ There is a distinction between the time of the episodes dominated by Clytemnestra—the real actor or doer of the play—and the time of the choral parodos and stasima. Here we have the contrast between a past condition or *status quo*—the war and its causes, the guilt of Agamemnon—and an incessant present activity, the hypocritical act of Clytemnestra. The distinction is expressed by the metrical difference between the lyric meters and the iambic trimeter. This differentiation of times is broken by the peculiar present-past-future time of Cassandra—the blend of retrospect and prophecy in a distended present, the unnatural interval when the murder hangs fire and the action is interrupted—and finally by the murder event itself that, in the final kommos and epirrhema between the chorus and Clytemnestra, creates another or fourth time, a direct combination or synthesis of past and future. What is decisive is the impact of the time of the episodes culminating in the murder—the great or decisive moment of the play—on the first time, or *status quo*. What teaches is not time in its progressive or unfolding aspect—as de Romilly would seem to think—but the momentary time of action, the action that breaks up the first "extended time" or *status quo* and creates the second "extended time" or *status quo*. ⟨. . .⟩

⟨. . .⟩ Aeschylus is primarily concerned with neither denouement nor pathos. This is why his "hero," Agamemnon, plays so small a part in the drama and his "villain," Clytemnestra, so large a one, or more exactly why Agamemnon is so largely subsumed in the lyric time of the choruses and kommoi and Clytemnestra is centered in the active time of the episodes. Agamemnon belongs to the old dispensation; Clytemnestra, to the moment that changes it. Once it is changed she reverts to the role of passive victim (in the *Choephoroe*). In Sophocles and Euripides the tragedy or suffering of the hero is *per se* determinative and crucial, while in Aeschyulus it is only a means to an end, a device that shifts one dispension into another. This means that Aeschylus' characters do not "count" in the manner of Sophoclean or Euripidean characters. Their guilt or innocence is important insofar as it affects the dispensation, not in respect to its own tragical or pathetic significance.

It is this difference that accounts for the unique relationship between chorus and episode that distinguishes Aeschylus. ⟨. . .⟩ Klaus Aichele has carefully diagrammed the relative length of episode (vis à vis parodoi, exodoi, and stasima) in the three tragedies: his analysis, even though in some vital respects incomplete, brings out clearly the unique standing of the *Oresteia* as compared with the dramas of either Sophocles or Euripides or the other dramas of Aeschylus. The *Agamemnon* is unique in the length of its parodos and first two stasima—more accurately in respect to the proportions of parodos, stasimon, and episode: a very long parodos followed by three stasima of decreasing length until the final, or third, stasimon approaches "normal" length. The lengthy and specialized character of its "fourth" episode and exodos is also unique. The shorter *Choephoroe* and *Eumenides* reveal a different arrangement, the former containing a first episode that embraces almost half the play, and the latter containing an exodos of disproportionate length. What dominate and are mainly responsible for the length of these sections—the fourth episode and exodos of the Agamemnon, the first episode of the *Choephoroe,* and the exodos of the *Eumenides*—are the kommoi and epirrhemata, or lyric and lyric-trimeter dialogues of chorus and actors (Cassandra, Clytemnestra, Electra, and Orestes, the Furies, and Athena). The centers of emphasis are those in which the action (represented by the actors) impinges on the "extended time" of the chorus and changes it to affect a new or different dispensation. The kommos is the crucial part of each play in the *Oresteia.* It is such by and through the way in which it "grows out" of the stasima and episodes. It is the place where the lyrical and dramatic elements of the drama are joined, where that third time—that past-future time as opposed to the past-present of the stasima and the mere present of the nonlyric episodes—is established.

> —Brooks Otis, *Cosmos & Tragedy: An Essay on the Meaning of Aeschylus* (Chapel Hill: University of North Carolina Press, 1981): pp. 58–60.

⟨֍⟩

TIMOTHY GANTZ ON AGAMEMNON'S INNOCENCE

[Timothy Gantz is Professor of Classics at the University of Georgia, and author of *Early Greek Myth: A Guide to Literary and Artistic Sources* (1993). Here, he asks us to reconsider whether Aeschylus does in fact visit the sins of his fathers (Atreus, Agamemnon) upon his sons (Agamemnon, Orestes).]

As ⟨Aigisthos⟩ presents the situation, Agamemnon has indeed atoned for the crimes of his father Atreus, and this is at least a sure reference to the *concept* of inherited guilt in Aischlos. But Aischylos himself is not speaking here, nor is Aigisthos what I would call an unbiased witness, any more than Agamemnon was. In point of fact the man is a usurper (as well as an adulterer), and it is in his interest to rationalize his position by whatever means he can. Since he has no claims against his cousin personally (nor it seems against his throne), he reaches back to a previous generation and tries to make the crimes of Atreus serve instead. The chorus, we may note, rejects completely this justification, just as they rejected Klytaimestra's claim that a *daimon* in her form committed the murder of her husband.

⟨. . .⟩ At *Agam.* the elders, caught between Kassandra's recent exit and Agamemnon's imminent death-cry, ponder further the meaning of what they have seen and heard. The gods, they say, have granted to their king to sack Troy, and to return home in honor; ⟨. . .⟩ "but if now he is to pay back the previous blood, and dying accomplish retribution to the dead for other deaths," who then will boast to be free of harm? Amid all the uncertain referents the crux of the wording is ⟨"previous blood"⟩: does this mean ⟨. . .⟩ the blood of previous generations? Or does it indicate, as Triklinios thought, the bloodshed of Agamemnon's own previous deeds, i.e. Iphigeneia (and perhaps others slain at Troy on his account)? Certainly either (or both) is possible, but the context of the chorus' thoughts seems to me to suggest more readily the latter. The elders have spent much of the play worrying about the consequences of Agamemnon's actions ⟨. . .⟩. Are we now to believe that they have totally forgotten this concern, decided that Agamemnon is essentially innocent, and chosen to anguish instead over the deeds of his ancestors, a subject which previously interested them not at all? ⟨. . .⟩

The other passage occurs near the end of the Eumenides, and carries the authority of no less a person than the goddess Athena. ⟨. . .⟩

"But he who comes upon these stern goddesses does not know from whence the blows of life strike him. For transgressions from former times lead him away to them." Here again, amid uncertainty as to whether the first line should be positive or negative, the crucial word is ⟨*proterōn*⟩, certainly rendered by most scholars as "forebears." But even if we accept an Aischylean belief in inherited guilt, I do not myself see what such a translation would mean at this point in the play. If Athena means to threaten evil-doers with the power of the Erinyes, the perspective should be that of the evil-doer, not his descendant. What is here gained by holding up fear of punishment before the innocent offspring who in retrospect can do nothing to alter the behavior of their guilty ancestors? Why, if Athena means to encourage more acceptable conduct by the citizens, does she not threaten the guilty themselves with future disasters for their race? ⟨. . .⟩ Moreover, we should remember that the nature of the Erinyes' jurisdiction, for purposes of this play at least, has centered on completely different concerns. The charge made by them against Orestes, and the only charge made by them, is one of personally committed matricide. In all their passionate arguments against the accused, and their desperation to secure a conviction, they never once suggest that in their eyes he could be guilty of the crimes of Atreus, or even of his father's slaying of Iphigeneia, though these are both deeds of kindred bloodshed. If the *Oresteia* is in any way about inherited guilt, surely we should expect that issue to be relevant here. ⟨. . .⟩

—Timothy Gantz, "Inherited Guilt in Aischylos," *Classical Journal* 78, no. 1 (1982): pp. 13–15.

Plot Summary of the
Choephori

In keeping with the *lex talionis,* Orestes must kill his father's killers. That one of them is his mother, however, means his story cannot follow standard lines of revenge-tragedy. Matricide is the profoundest defilement of nature, transmuting the very fount of life and fertility into barrenness and death; Euripides' Clytemnestra "carried her own death in her womb." And this dilemma forms the center of *Oresteia*'s chaos: "Vengeance is matricide, vengeance is just" (Anne Lebeck).

The first two plays of the trilogy are stylistically very different: Leon Golden has proposed that the technique of *Choephori* is essentially symbolist, in marked contrast with the psychological drama of *Agamemnon.* Yet both plays treat of homecoming and murder, and the parallelism of Orestes' act with Clytemnestra's reinforces their equivalence. (The Chorus will remind us that the shedding of blood, like the loss of virginity, is irrevocable: Every life must be paid by another life, and so the chain of retaliation never can end.) Repetition also occurs within the play, as when the Chorus' instruction of Electra at the opening prefigures their encouragement of Orestes in the *commos. Choephori* is a play of mirrors.

Orestes' revenge is the only legend we know to have been dramatized by all three of the great tragic playwrights. Sophocles and Euripides each wrote an *Electra,* Euripides an additional *Orestes.* Aeschylus, by contrast, names his play collectively after Electra and her slave women—perhaps to implicate them as its prime movers. Indeed, while the play opens on Orestes, he has time only to dedicate a lock of hair before the libation-bearers approach, and they are to dominate much of the action to come.

As Orestes looks on, the Chorus offer lengthy prayers for the murdered king, condemning "that godless woman," Clytemnestra. The pride of Argos, we learn, has gone; though Agamemnon's tomb still looms over the set, and will play a role of its own in advancing the plot.

Electra describes how Clytemnestra has sent her to offer libations—libations which, as she knows, are in no way sincere ("Shall I say bring him love for love, a woman's / love for husband? My mother, love from her?"). The Chorus tell her to honor Aegisthus' enemies with the blessing: The Chorus Leader, rather than Electra, is first to speak Orestes' name. Line by line, she instructs the girl in calling for vengeance on her father's killers, reminding her of the debt of blood ("How now, / and pay the enemy back in kind?"). Electra appeals explicitly to Agamemnon, and stress is laid on herself and Orestes as—like their father—helpless victims of the monstrous Clytemnestra.

The libations complete, Electra now discovers Orestes' lock of hair. The ensuing "recognition scene" has been criticized for its baroqueness, as Electra compares first the hair, then the footprints to her own. Fitting her own feet to the steps, she is led by them to, of course, Orestes—yet she continues to doubt his identity until shown a piece of weaving. Jørgen Mejer suggests that the weaving operates not only as recognition-sign but also as a reminder that, unlike Clytemnestra, Electra has performed intimate domestic acts for her brother in younger days. The reunion is a glad one—since, as Electra says, they have no family left but each other—and together the two address invocations to Zeus, begging his aid in their vengeance.

Electra's "But if we are to live and reach the haven, / one small seed could grow a mighty tree—" is picked up by Orestes, who stresses his father's heroism and the "proud dynastic tree" nearly "ruined" by the devouring woman. Encouraged by the Chorus, he describes how Apollo himself decreed retaliation against Clytemnestra. There is a mention of Furies, but they are Agamemnon's, not hers: Pollution, insanity, and exile await Orestes if he fails. Moreover, Orestes has motives of his own for killing: A usurper holds his throne; he grieves for his father; and he is repulsed at the thought of Troy's heroes "[going] at the beck and call of a brace of women" (i.e., Clytemnestra and Aegisthus).

There now begins the *commos*, a prolonged invocation of Agamemnon's spirit. Orestes has, of course, already determined to avenge father and city. But the *commos*, besides summoning "the dark gods beneath the earth," must serve also to steel Orestes' nerve.

Goaded by the chorus, the children's cries become more and more bloodthirsty. Stress is laid on Agamemnon's might and heroism ("king of kings,"), and—again—on the mere "remnant" left of his house. Notably, Orestes and the Chorus alike avoid the word "mother"; Electra does use it, but in direct passionate rebuke of a woman who has earned her fate. Clytemnestra, after all, not only killed her husband, but mutilated his corpse and buried it unmourned; she betrayed even the bonds of motherhood in adulterous love for Aegisthus. The image of the net that trapped Agamemnon is finally made an augury of hope by the Chorus Leader, who compares avenging children to corks keeping a net afloat. Thus Agamemnon's rescue is not merely a duty for Orestes and Electra, but proceeds from their very nature as a father's children.

The *commos* complete, Orestes asks what had prompted the sending of libations, and is given the account of "Clytemnestra's dream." Clytemnestra saw herself bear a snake; milk mixed with blood when she gave it suck, and she awoke in fear. Orestes without hesitation accepts the dream's forecast: "I turn serpent. / I kill her. So the vision says." Perhaps to heighten suspense, Aeschylus has Orestes propose an approach to the palace which ultimately will not be used. The "third libation" of the *Agamemnon* resurfaces in his description of the blood he will shed for Zeus. And the Chorus describe Althaia, Scylla, and the Lemnian women, criminal females whose example is given to ready us for Clytemnestra's death.

Orestes knocks at the gate, representing himself to the Porter as a stranger from Daulis. Clytemnestra, failing to recognize her son, greets him warmly and speaks (with unconscious irony!) of the "warm baths" and hospitality of the house. She professes grief at the news of "Orestes'" death; but Orestes' nurse, Cilissa, immediately appears to give the lie to her maternal protestations.

Disparaging the queen's grief, Cilissa remembers how it was she, and not his mother, who had cared for the young Orestes. The Chorus Leader convinces her to suppress part of Clytemnestra's summons, so that Aegisthus will come unguarded. When he arrives, Aegisthus is easily dispatched; the queen, who instantly grasps the riddle that "The dead are killing the living," calls for "an axe to kill a man."

Confronted by her son, Clytemnestra makes a last appeal, asking if he can have no pity for the breast that suckled him into life. Orestes is finally unnerved by the enormity of what he must do, and begs help of Pylades, only now using the word "mother." His companion answers with his only lines in the play: "What of the Prophet God Apollo, / the Delphic voice, the faiths and oaths we swear? / Make all mankind your enemy, not the gods." Pylades functions essentially as the god's proxy, and his words are enough to sway Orestes, who prepares to kill his mother over her lover's corpse. Agamemnon may, he acknowledges, have brought his own death upon himself, but now so has Clytemnestra: "You killed and it was outrage—suffer outrage now."

The Chorus offer thanksgiving at the restoration of Agamemnon's house: "[S]oon Time will stride through the gates with blessings, / once the hearth burns off corruption, once / the house drives off the Furies." They little doubt the siege will be lifted, but as their song ends the doors reopen to the trilogy's second murder tableau—an uncanny bookend to the first.

Orestes displays the robe that caught Agamemnon, reminding his audience of his mother's sin and justifying his work before the Sun itself. "I pursued this bloody death with justice, / *mother's* death." He feels nothing for the death of Aegisthus, but, as he contemplates Clytemnestra's murder, his certainty—and sanity—waver. "[S]uffering is just about to bloom," warn the Chorus, and Orestes' visions become more and more disjointed. A "charioteer" bound to a harness of pain, he finally sees his only hope in purification by Apollo at Delphi.

The Chorus try to reassure him of the justice of his act, but suddenly Orestes is beset by visions of his mother's Furies. Though the Leader believes them to be mere hallucination, the monsters "thick and fast, / their eyes dripping hate" are only too real to Orestes, whom they chase off the stage. The play ends on a representative and questioning note: "Where will it end?— / where will it sink to sleep and rest, / this murderous hate, this Fury?" ❀

List of Characters in the
Choephori

Orestes has returned from exile to avenge Agamemnon and reclaim his birthright. But the pound of flesh due his father means he must outrage nature by killing his mother; and when he does, he is beset by madness. Some critics find evidence of the trilogy's moral evolution in the contrast between Orestes' reluctance in *Choephori* and Clytemnestra's blood-thirst in *Agamemnon*.

Pylades, an Aeschylean "silent actor," accompanies Orestes throughout the play, but speaks only once. Brooks Otis notes that while Orestes "steels himself for the deed (Schadewaldt) and even begins to accept its guilt (Lesky) ⟨. . .⟩ the moment of action shows that he does not accept it, that he has to be urged on by the voice of Apollo speaking through Pylades."

Electra with the encouragement of the Chorus, helps spur her brother to revenge. She is motivated by love for her dead father and by resentment of her mother; Orestes' vengeance will also enable her to marry. Her frenzied appeals to her father's spirit become extremely bloodthirsty, though, unlike the *Agamemnon*'s Clytemnestra, she voices an explicit concern for purity.

Chorus and Leader a group of slave-women who, according to Marsh McCall, probably grew up in Argos, though many have assumed they were captured at Troy. Unlike most choruses, they intervene directly in the action, not only goading the children's revenge but also persuading Cilissa to suppress a message. Their importance is underscored by the naming of Aeschylus' play after the "libation-bearers."

Orestes' knocking and call for "a man inside the house" are answered by a **Porter** who opens the gates.

Plagued by bad dreams, **Clytemnestra** sends libations to appease Agamemnon; her hypocrisy backfires when Electra and Orestes meet at the tomb. Though the *commos* systematically erodes her status as wife and mother, Clytemnestra remains a formidable opponent, and very nearly faces down her son. The threat of her Furies fails to sway Orestes, who if he does not kill her will anyway be dogged by Agamemnon's.

The charming, bumbling nurse **Cilissa** appears to reminisce fondly of Orestes' youth. Her somewhat lengthy scene serves to briefly ease the tension of the plot, and also to undercut Clytemnestra's claims to motherhood. The Chorus later persuade her to alter a summons so that Aegisthus will arrive unarmed.

Aegisthus plays an even smaller role in *Choephori* than he did in *Agamemnon.* Fiercely resented by the king's children, he is easily dispatched. Orestes loses his sanity on killing his mother, but feels no qualms at the execution of Aegisthus: Greek custom held it acceptable to kill an adulterer.

Aegisthus' **Servant** has only a bit part in *Choephori,* reacting with due horror to his master's death. Though previously fooled by Orestes' disguise, Clytemnestra immediately understands his cry—"The dead are killing the living"—to mean that her son has come to kill her. ❀

Critical Views on the
Choephori

ANNE LEBECK ON THE *COMMOS*

[Anne Lebeck was Associate Professor of Classics at Amherst College. She is the author of *The Oresteia: A Study in Language and Structure* (1971) and of several influential articles. Here, she examines the uses and form of the *commos,* tracing the invocation's slow crescendo of language and urgency as it "explores two aspects of the coming action: vengeance is matricide, vengeance is just."]

⟨. . .⟩ Explaining why "this deed must be done" there is one reason which Orestes does not give: the law of Dikē, demands it. In the commos, from their opening anapests, the chorus instruct him in this law. ⟨. . .⟩

⟨H⟩e experiences the intense emotion accompanying such insight, the ⟨*pathos*⟩ which culminates in ⟨*mathos*⟩. And at the end he restates his decision in terms of Dikē: Right will clash with Right. ⟨. . .⟩ "Orestes' dilemma" is not presented as moral revulsion from Apollo's command. Rather it is the problem posed by an act simultaneously right and wrong. ⟨. . .⟩

As invocation hymn the commos has a double purpose: to awaken the wrath of the dead king and, simultaneously, that of his living avenger. ⟨. . .⟩

⟨T⟩he commos is a cry of despair at once ritual and personal.

The very structure of the lyric reflects movement toward renewed resolve, suggests doubt overcome. The first section is triadic and epirrhematic. In each of the four triads a choral strophe of encouragement is surrounded by the despairing strophe and antistrophe of Orestes and Electra. The effect is that of a vicious circle. The triads are punctuated by three anapestic epirrhemata, probably delivered by the coryphaeus, which add further exhortation. Thus the form is ABA-epirrhema-CBC-epirrhema-DED-epirrhema-FEF. The first triad (ABA) is closely connected with the second (CBC) both formally (by response of B, the choral strophe) and by similarity of content. The same close relation obtains between the third and fourth triads, which mark increase of confidence on the part of Orestes. The second epirrhema serves as a dividing line between the first two triads and the second two. Its importance in changing the attitude of Orestes and Electra is underlined by length (eight as opposed to the five lines of its fellows) and a more complex metrical pattern.

In the second section Electra, herself convinced, joins forces with the chorus. One after another they urge Orestes. The preceding triadic form gives way to a strophic pair of three stanzas each, the strophes of brother and sister no longer in responsion. Form: A (chorus) B (Electra) C (Orestes) // C (Chorus) A (Electra) B (Chorus). Here Orestes regains his purpose, repeats his decision with new intensity.

In the third and last section Orestes, Electra, and the chorus form a single will, united by the desire for vengeance. The first strophic pair consists of a line delivered by Orestes, one by Electra, and three by the chorus. The last strophe and antistrophe are sung by the chorus alone. The despair which they now voice at the curse upon Agamemnon's house echoes the earlier despair of Orestes at his own dilemma, the climax of that curse. An actual attempt to conjure up the ghost does not begin until after the commos and is performed by Orestes and Electra alone. The chorus retire to the background, their task accomplished.

Another line of development ⟨runs⟩ parallel with that discussed above ⟨. . .⟩. During the lyric the justice of vengeance is set forth; at the same time this just vengeance reveals itself as matricide, a greater crime than that which it must punish. The figure of Clytemnestra is slowly detached from Aegisthus until at last she stands alone, true object of the coming retribution. ⟨. . .⟩

In the earlier decision Orestes does not refer to Clytemnestra as his mother or speak of her alone. He calls the murderers "two women." Such plurals are used consistently throughout the early scenes and at the beginning of the commos ⟨. . .⟩. The relationship of child and parent then rises slowly to the surface. ⟨. . .⟩

Scholarly opinion on the meaning of line 385 is sharply divided. Should ⟨tokeusi⟩ be taken as a "true plural, in a general statement; whatever is meant by the whole phrase is true for parents as for others, or is true for the guilty, parents though they may be"? If, instead, the plural is used for singular, does it refer to the mother

(Blass, Blaydes, Mazon, Rose, Werner) or the father (Lesky, Schade-waldt, the scholiast, Smyth, Wilamowitz)? Or could there be a refer-ence to punishment as child of crime, the offspring resembling its parent (Tucker, Verrall?)

In their efforts to determine the exact meaning, commentators have overlooked one point: what is the function of a line that lends itself so well to antithetical interpretations (father/mother)? Although ⟨tokeus⟩ means "father" in the singular, the plural means not "fathers" but "parents," father and mother together. ⟨Tokeusi th' omos teleitai⟩ applies to both parents: fulfillment of revenge for the father, for the mother penalty paid in full. And this is the dilemma of Orestes. The task of avenging his father entails wronging his mother; he cannot do one without the other.

—Anne Lebeck, *The Oresteia: A Study in Language and Structure* (Washington: Center for Hellenic Studies, 1971): pp. 113–16, 118.

⟨⟩

BRIAN VICKERS ON CLYTEMNESTRA'S RETREAT

[Brian Vickers is Chair of English Literature at the Centre for Renaissance Studies at the Swiss Federal Institute of Tech-nology in Zürich. His books include *Francis Bacon and Renaissance Prose* (1968), *In Defense of Rhetoric* (1988), and *Appropriating Shakespeare: Contemporary Critical Quarrels* (1993). Below he shows how, to prepare us for Clytemnestra's entrance and murder, Aeschylus gradually strips her of her moral authority as a mother (while simultaneously rein-stating the fallen Agamemnon as father and war-hero).]

⟨. . .⟩ He is no longer a figure of guilt, for Iphigenia is only mentioned once in the play and then from the viewpoint of Electra's love for her family, not of Agamemnon's sacrifice of his daughter. ⟨. . .⟩ Orestes and the Chorus lament that he did not die a hero's death at Troy ⟨. . .⟩.

⟨. . .⟩ 'How shall we be lords in our own house?' asks Electra. 'We have been sold, and go as wanderers because our mother bought herself, for us, a man'. Yet, she says, before she knows that Orestes has come home,

if we are to win, and our ship live,
from one small seed could burgeon an enormous tree. ⟨...⟩

⟨M⟩etaphors and symbols express, over and over again, the unity of the family and the processes of procreation, generation, transmission. ⟨...⟩

⟨...⟩ Since Agamemnon is represented by such phallic images as the growing tree, and his children are his seeds, then Clytemnestra is the force which would destroy the phallus, destroy procreation, make the seeds barren. We recall her appalling exultation over Agamemnon's death, ⟨...⟩ For her, death of the man is life. ⟨...⟩

⟨...⟩ The Chorus declares that, compared to the destructive forces of nature, nothing is more formidable than the pride of men or 'the desperate passions/of women without scruple': ⟨...⟩

The theme of this strophe might be described as 'female love of mastery', that which has driven Clytemnestra all along. Now the Chorus moves to myths which illustrate this process. ⟨...⟩

The structure of Aeschylus' choric odes is not one of logical sequence: rather, successive strophes illuminate different facets, or work by juxtaposition. Here the myth links up with the masculine imagery already discussed, with the symbol of the staff or sceptre (here, torch) planted in the hearth (here, womb) As we recall, Althaea killed her son Meleager by burning the torch on which his life depended. The male stem was destroyed by the female.

In this strophe, as in the antistrophe following, we are given an account of a crime against the closest of human relationships. ⟨...⟩ The third strophe contains a remarkable surprise. Aeschylus has set up the familiar structure of mythical parallels, each reflecting back on the subject which is being illuminated by the analogies. Now he suddenly inserts the subject itself among the analogies as the Chorus sing of Aegisthus and Clytemnestra. ⟨...⟩

⟨T⟩his is a brilliant conflation of myth with reality, and with the moral structure of violation common to both. It also shows Aeschylus' suggestive juxtaposition of myths in order to superimpose one image on another, or make one image evoke related types of action—a form of ethical *montage* of myths. ⟨...⟩

⟨I⟩n the third antistrophe Aeschylus returns to myth ⟨...⟩.

⟨The crime of the women of Lemnos⟩ led to a land without men. And that, he suggests, is the situation which applies in the palace at Argos. ⟨...⟩

Aeschylus' second undermining of Clytemnestra in advance of a crucial scene is related to the building up of her unnaturalness, and involves the Nurse ⟨...⟩.

⟨...⟩ There are still some critics who think that this scene is a charming, if irrelevant, piece of folk humour, but it ought to be obvious that it relates to the issues of inheritance and parentage which are so vital in this play. The last references to a mother's milk and a baby's insides were in the fable of the lion cub: this passage stands as a total contrast to that. I cannot agree with Bernard Knox that that fable also applies to Orestes, for he grows up not to 'ruin his house' but to reclaim it, and the oppressive weight of disaster and pollution will be lifted by him. ⟨...⟩ ⟨T⟩he care of the Nurse represents genuine human love, and it produces the same qualities in Orestes, who will destroy their perversion by Clytemnestra. The parallel acts, once again, to spotlight a crucial difference. If the lion cub 'showed the temper it had from its parents', then it is clear that Orestes has escaped all the evil and distortion of Clytemnestra and has only inherited the good qualities of his father. That wholly admirable picture of Agamemnon built up since the Cassandra scene has become a valid model. ⟨...⟩

In addition to stressing the different *ethos* which Orestes has inherited, this scene calls in question Clytemnestra's status as a mother, diminishing it almost to vanishing point. ⟨...⟩

—Brian Vickers, *Towards Greek Tragedy: Drama, Myth, Society* (London: Longman, 1973): pp. 394, 397–404.

❧

STANLEY IRELAND ON STICHOMYTHIA

[Stanley Ireland is a Senior Lecturer in Classics and Ancient History at the University of Warwick. He is the author of *Roman Britain: A Sourcebook* (1986), and of translations of *Terence's Hecyra* (1990) and *Menander of Athens' Dyscolus*

(1995). This extract analyzes Aeschylus' use of line-by-line dialogue to emphasize the sympathy (or antipathy) between speaking characters, establishing "contact on an intellectual as well as structural level."]

Contact but no sympathy can be seen ⟨. . .⟩ at the end of the *Agamemnon* in the confrontation between Aegisthus and the chorus. Contact in the form of give and take is beyond doubt, but once more there are few connecting particles, especially as tempers rise towards the close: The two sides are not interested in answering what the other has to say, merely in the production of counter statements; they stand apart hurling threats and abuse. ⟨. . .⟩

Elsewhere the lack of sympathetic contact between the parties engaged in stichomythia is relaxed to meet the needs of the moment. So for instance one character may attempt to draw the other, unwilling, into a similar frame of mind, or into the adoption of a similar course of action. The result in many cases is a one-sided attempt to maintain dramatic and syntactic contact in the face of continuous resistance, as in the dialogue between Clytemnestra and Agamemnon. ⟨. . .⟩ He has no desire to converse at length or even at times to continue the exchange. The result is an almost total lack of connecting particles in his lines, an indication of how grudging are his replies. Clytemnestra, on the other hand ⟨. . .⟩ has a vested interest in maintaining contact. ⟨. . .⟩

⟨. . .⟩ This same characteristic occurs again, notably in the third passage of stichomythia between Cassandra and the chorus. In continuing the theme with which she closed her last rhesis, the prophetess shows every indication of becoming resigned to her fate, so much so that she begins to lose awareness of her surroundings, engrossed instead in the past and the atmosphere of death that hangs heavily over the House of Atreus. As a result her lines are devoid of connecting particles, while in contrast the chorus strives to halt her path towards inevitable death. ⟨. . .⟩

The force of interest which prompts a character to maintain and actively foster contact ⟨. . .⟩ need not be one purely of curiosity; indignation too may produce a similar effect. So at Choephoroe, where Orestes reveals his identity, the particles come consistently from Electra, alarmed at the intrusion of this supposed stranger and seeking an explanation for it ⟨. . .⟩.

⟨. . .⟩ Clytemnestra's attempt to ward off her death at the hands of her son ⟨. . .⟩ opens with the refutation of her case; the connectives come from Orestes, who pounces upon his mother's words to render them invalid by addition. ⟨. . .⟩

⟨W⟩here Electra questions the chorus on the words she should use in offering the libation to her dead father, the ⟨. . .⟩ technique of syntactic union to indicate sympathetic co-operation is conspicuous. ⟨. . .⟩ Likewise in the Commos she combines with Orestes in a complicated invocation of Agamemnon, made all the more effective by its central position and the symmetry of the surrounding area ⟨. . .⟩. Later still two instances of hypotactic linking occur in the description of Clytemnestra's dream. Indeed it is not to be wondered at that in a play where so much of the action is made to hinge upon the co-operation of the various characters, that this same co-operation should extend also to the structure of the language.

By contrast, the *Eumenides* sees a return to a less extreme pattern of occurrence, and to a usage of hypotactic linking which owes more to the formalistic requirements of achieving brevity of expression. In the exchange between Athena and the Erinyes the instances are the result not so much of sympathy or the need for logical connection, but like Persae or Agamemnon, a simple and effective means of presenting complex ideas within the framework of poetic form.

—Stanley Ireland, "Stichomythia in Aeschylus: The Dramatic Role of Syntax and Connecting Particles," *Hermes* 102, no. 4 (1974): pp. 515–18, 520.

⊛

A. F. Garvie on Plot and Suspense in the *Choephori*

[A. F. Garvie was Chair of the Department of Classics at the University of Glasgow. He is the author of a translation of Sophocles' *Ajax* (1998), and a commentary on the *Choephori* (1986). Here, he shows how Aeschylus frustrates audience expectations (for example, by twice reversing the anticipated order of the killings) in order both to dramatize Orestes' moral uncertainty and also heighten suspense.]

⟨. . .⟩ Lesky has shown how every time the vengeance is referred to it is in curiously vague terms, and in particular Clytaemestra is rarely mentioned. It is Aegisthus who is named, and the scene before the ⟨commos⟩ ends, as Lesky emphasises, with Aegisthus firmly fixed in our minds. Above all in the central ⟨commos⟩ it is only at the climax of the whole composition that Orestes says directly that his mother will pay for the dishonour done to his father, though even here he does not use the word⟨mētēr⟩. ⟨. . .⟩

Orestes interprets ⟨Clytemnestra's dream⟩ to mean that he will kill his mother. Everything follows on naturally from his statement. Then comes a surprise. Orestes outlines his plan to Electra and the Chorus. He and Pylades will come to the palace-door disguised as guest-friends and speaking in Phocian accents, and, if they are not admitted, they will wait outside until Aegisthus is shamed into receiving them. Once inside he imagines either that he will find Aegisthus sitting on Agamemnon's throne, or that Aegisthus will come in later and send for him. In either case Orestes will kill him immediately. Nothing is said about the killing of Clytaemestra. It has long been a source of puzzlement that few of the details of this plan are in fact to be fulfilled. ⟨. . .⟩ Why does Aeschylus apparently waste time in contriving a plan which seems to be dramatically so irrelevant? ⟨. . .⟩ When the plan is not fulfilled it comes as a surprise, and there may be no more to it than that. Better still will be to show that the speech does contribute to the dramatic climax of the play. Its peculiarity may be summed up briefly by saying that it concentrates entirely on Aegisthus and almost totally ignores Clytaemestra. This, like the ⟨commos⟩, may be interpreted in terms of Orestes' character. Once he has made up his mind to kill his mother he withdraws again from his commitment and prefers to think of the killing of Aegisthus. It may equally well be seen in terms of the audience's expectation. As the scene ends, and the Chorus prepare to sing the first stasimon, it is the killing of Aegisthus that we expect to come first. ⟨. . .⟩

Having so carefully established this expectation in our minds Aeschylus proceeds immediately in the first stasimon to return us to uncertainty. The Chorus compare the murder of Agamemnon with various mythical crimes, a common factor of which is that they were committed by women against male relations. They are obviously thinking of Clytaemestra, and now it seems to be Aegisthus who is forgotten. ⟨. . .⟩ When therefore the stasimon ends and Orestes knocks on the palace-door, with the words ⟨tis enthon?⟩ the audience genuinely does not know the answer. ⟨. . .⟩ Orestes tells the servant to announce his arrival to the ⟨kyrioi dōmatōn⟩, and we note the vague masculine plural. Three leisurely lines keep us in suspense, until he suggests that a ⟨dōmatōn telesphoros gyne⟩ should come out, and we think of Clytaemestra, whom the description fits so well. But immediately he goes on to say, in the next three and a half lines, that he would rather deal with a man, and it looks as if Aegisthus indeed will be the first to emerge. ⟨. . .⟩ It leads up most effectively to the tremendous moment when the door finally opens, and it is after all not Aegisthus but Clytaemestra who appears. ⟨. . .⟩ Now at last Orestes confronts his mother, and the audience must feel with a shock that the matricide will follow. It is a moment of supreme tension. But again Aeschylus frustrates us; for this first confrontation takes a very different form from matricide. In the middle of the scene Orestes tells his lying tale, and this, together with Clytaemestra's reaction to it, is framed by the elaborate, but also sinister, courtesies of hospitality offered and received. The tension relaxes as we remember that no plan has been made for Clytaemestra's murder. Aegisthus after all is to be dealt with first. The scene ends with the Nurse sent to fetch him.

The second stasimon is filled with prayers to various deities for help in the coming struggle. Towards the end we have a clear allusion to Clytaemestra. Despite the uncertainties of the text it is plain enough that the Chorus visualise the scene of matricide, with Clytaemestra addressing her son as ⟨teknon⟩. Orestes is to resist her appeals and to have a heart like that of Perseus, who, the audience will remember, turned away his face when killing Medusa. Once more we forget about Aegisthus, and we wonder if Clytaemestra after all is to be the first victim. ⟨. . .⟩ It is only when the stasimon finishes that we catch sight of Aegisthus coming up the parodos, and we realise, again with a surprise, that he is to be dealt with first. ⟨. . .⟩

—A. F. Garvie, "Aeschylus' Simple Plots," in *Dionysiaca : Nine Studies in Greek Poetry by Former Pupils, Presented to Sir Denys Page on His Seventieth Birthday,* eds. R. D. Dawe, J. Diggle, and P. E. Easterling (Cambridge: Cambridge University Library, 1978): pp. 77–80.

[Oliver Taplin is Professor of Classics at Magdalen College, Oxford. His books include *The Stagecraft of Aeschylus: The Dramatic Use of Exits and Entrances in Greek Tragedy* (1977), *Homeric Soundings: The Shaping of the* Iliad (1992), and *Comic Angels and Other Approaches to Greek Drama Through Vase Paintings* (1993). Below, he explains how—and why—Clytemnestra's murder is staged as a deliberate echo of Agamemnon's.]

⟨. . .⟩ The hint of repetition ⟨. . .⟩ returns with more force and clarity in the later scene. Once more a man and a woman argue about going into the palace, and once more what is at stake is mortal victory and defeat. For the stage movement of the exit means death for one of the two at the other's hand. Again the dispute takes the form of a line-by-line dialogue between the two actors (a rare technique in Aeschylus, where dialogue between the chorus and an actor is the norm). Clytemnestra, like Agamenon, eventually gives way, and at the end of the scene the victim is accompanied by the slaughterer into the house. But the significance of the mirror scene is now more disturbing than the earlier scenes, for the similarities of the situations blend with and stain the differences. There are differences: in *Cho* the situation is open and honest unlike the lavish and contorted ambiguities in *Agam.* Orestes bluntly perseveres with a task which distresses him, unlike Clytemnestra who gloatingly indulged her calculated murderousness. Orestes recognizes the moral duality of his situation; he does not deny that a mother as well as a father may invoke wrathful hounds of vengeance. And his last words as he takes her in are 'You killed one you should not have killed: now suffer what you should not suffer' (a single line in Greek!). And this is where the similarities come into view again. The parties have changed, a new generation is involved, yet the deed is the same. We are now too near the actual shedding of blood to turn a blind eye to the repetitiveness of the situation. Killing is killing, kin is kin. This begins to prepare us for the turn of events in the last part of the play.

Lastly, and most strikingly, there is the visual correspondence of the two murder tableaux. ⟨. . .⟩

⟨. . .⟩ It is not certain how the scene in *Agam* was staged, but however it was done, there can be no doubt that the tableau at *Cho* was staged in exactly the same way. Once more the murderer stands, blood on his hands, by the corpses of a man and a woman, lovers. Once more the murderer stands up for the deed. And, above all, there once more is the robe-net which was wrapped round Agamemnon— now, like other things in *Cho,* brought out into the open. Orestes has it held up for all to see ⟨. . .⟩.

⟨. . .⟩ The similarities are too pressing, too close: the mind goes straight back to *Agam.* The blood feud is repeating itself, it is self-perpetuating. Despite the optimism which has run through *Cho,* especially in the last choral song, this new realization of repetitiveness is quickly reflected in the ambivalence of the chorus' first reaction:

> For him who is still here suffering also begins to bloom. . . .
> One ordeal here today: another is still to come tomorrow. ⟨. . .⟩

Yet there are still differences. Above all, Orestes has the express sanction of Apollo, and hence of Zeus. And this is brought out by a new—and therefore intrusive—visual element in the tableau in *Cho.* In one hand Orestes probably holds his sword, which marks him as like Clytemnestra: but in the other he has a suppliant's branch and wreath:

> And that is why you see me here, equipped
> with this branch bound with wool. I shall appeal
> to Apollo's sanctuary, a suppliant. . . .

⟨. . .⟩ In a mirror scene any difference will stand out in the repeated surroundings; so in *Cho* the branch and wreath draw the eye as a signpost to the future.

> —Oliver Taplin, *Greek Tragedy in Action* (Berkeley: University of California Press, 1978): pp. 124–26.

⟨ॐ⟩

A. L. Brown on Orestes' Madness

[A. L. Brown is Director of Humanities Publishing at the Cambridge University Press. He is the author of *A New*

Companion to Greek Tragedy (1983), and of editions of Sophocles' *Antigone* (1987) and George Eliot's *Romola* (1993). In this extract, he examines the inconsistency between the Furies as they first appear to Orestes in the *Choephori* (as a symptom of the madness that might realistically attend upon a matricide) and as they occur in the *Eumenides* (as physically incarnate spirits whose aim is to *cause* the now-sane Orestes to go mad).]

⟨. . .⟩ We have seen that the first stage in the development of Orestes' madness is a sequence of ideas in his mind, rather obscure in detail but centered on the murderous robe, proceeding through grief for his father to grief at all the crimes of the family and a sense of his own pollution; that this was followed by the first stirrings of madness, described in subjective and psychological terms; that this in turn was followed by a vision of the Furies, which was the symptom of madness; and that it accordingly seemed reasonable for the Chorus-leader to describe this vision as a mere fantasy. Thus, while I have always tried to proceed impartially from the text, I have felt able at each stage to stress a quality that must be called realism or naturalism. Aeschylus has been presenting, through the conventions of Greek tragedy, not a miraculous and impossible event—a man set upon by mythical monsters—but one that could plausibly happen in real life—a man passing from sanity to madness. ⟨. . .⟩

⟨. . .⟩ Aeschylus need not have written the scene as he did. Orestes' defense of his deed could have been followed immediately by the direct intervention of the Furies, and his madness could either have come after this intervention or have gone unmentioned altogether. In either case the Furies would have seemed much more like pure mumbo-jumbo, as they may well have done in earlier poetry. Their connection with madness does not seem inevitable, for a belief in avenging demons could presumably have arisen simply from people's horror at certain types of crime, from the victim's desire that his curses should be visited on the criminal, and from the criminal's fear that they might. This is confirmed by the nature of the Erinyes in Homer, which work purely by overdetermining 'natural' events; ⟨. . .⟩

I have not yet discussed the reason *why* Aeschylus should have abandoned the human viewpoint of *Ag.* and *Cho.* when he came to *Eum.*, given that that viewpoint enabled him to be true to life without in any way preventing him from exploring the religious implications of the action, and given the sacrifice of strict consistency which the change entails. ⟨. . .⟩

I offer, however, a few subjective comments. *Ag.* and *Cho.* present us with a problem that is strictly insoluble in its own terms: the doer must suffer, and therefore crime must breed further crime in an endless cycle. ⟨. . .⟩ ⟨I⟩f the gods had simply burst miraculously into the world of *Cho.* to end the sequence of evil by their own arbitrary decree, the audience would have felt cheated and the issues of the first two plays would have been intolerably trivialised. The same would have been true, I think, if the human agents had suddenly found that they could somehow solve the problem by themselves. Aeschylus wants to preserve the serious, 'tragic' vision of *Ag.* and *Cho.*, but he also wants, however illogically, to end the trilogy on a note of joy and hope, which expresses, perhaps, an emotional faith in what might be (the blessings bestowed on Athens at the end are to be fulfilled from 458 BC on) rather than a belief about existing reality. The impossible is achieved partly through the complexities and ambiguities of the Trial Scene (the equal vote showing that the insoluble problems of *Ag.* and *Cho.* are not forgotten), but partly also, I believe, through the deliberate alteration, at the beginning of *Eum.*, of the very premises on which the action rests; for, once the issue has been turned into a conflict between divine powers on stage, this can be resolved by the defeat and conversion of one party. ⟨. . .⟩

When Beethoven wrote symphonies in minor keys but wanted to end them joyfully in the major, he similarly faced the problem of achieving this without negating and trivialising the 'tragic' vision of the earlier movements. In both the Fifth and the Ninth Symphonies he sought to solve this problem by providing self-conscious transition passages to show that the finale stands in some peculiar relation (however this is to be defined) to what has gone before, and also by altering his very medium (adding new instruments in the Fifth and a choir and soloists in the Ninth) to show that the music is moving to a different plane. Parallels between different artistic forms can never take us far, but there may be some force in this one.

—A. L. Brown, "The Erinyes in the *Oresteia*," *Journal of Hellenic Studies* 103 (1983): pp. 20–21, 33–34.

⟨♥⟩

[Marsh McCall is Professor of Classics at Stanford University. He has written *Ancient Rhetorical Theories of Simile and Comparison* (1969), and edited *Aeschylus: A Collection of Critical Essays* (1972). Here, he spotlights a discrepancy between the chorus' status (as female slaves of the household) and their manner (as before-the-fact accomplices to matricide).]

What the chorus chant and sing in the *kommos* is consistent with their overall structural dominance. They immediately set a tone of unrelenting vengeance in the introductory anapaests, ("as she demands her due, loud cries the voice of Justice"). And as soon as Orestes has delivered his first stanza they address him as ⟨*teknon*⟩, and rather than reflecting deferentially on what he has just sung, they start to lecture and exhort him. Throughout the *kommos* the chorus steadily remain initiator, adviser, and inciter to Electra and Orestes; the children *never* ask or direct the chorus to follow or support *their* lead. ⟨...⟩

⟨...⟩ An audience would not expect the Nurse to be subservient to the chorus' wishes. Cilissa is an old, loyal, trusted personal servant, surely with a standing at least that of a group of palace slaves. She has a name, something extremely unusual in tragedy for anyone of low status. Eurycleia and Phaedra's Nurse remind us that nurse-figures could exert considerable authority and independence. And yet the anonymous chorus through their anonymous leader dominate and direct Cilissa, severely charging her to ensure that Aegisthus comes alone. Further, as often noted, Aeschylus has *created* this piece of plot interference; it was not forced upon him. ⟨...⟩

After the murders, as the final scene begins, Orestes reemerges from the palace, displaying the bodies of Clytemnestra and Aegisthus. In a series of three speeches separated by two sets of choral anapaests, Orestes attempts to defend his deeds and determine his next course of action, but feels himself slipping into madness. To whom does he make his appeals? ⟨...⟩ Many commentators ⟨...⟩ bring onto the stage at 973 a silent group of Argives to provide the appropriate audience for Orestes. ⟨...⟩ Both Taplin and Garvie, however, among others, reject decisively, and rightly, such a premise and regard the chorus as the sole recipients of Orestes' words (except for one or more attendants who bear Agamemnon's robe and are addressed).

This leaves the female slave chorus in a remarkable position. ⟨. . .⟩ What Aeschylus has done quite deliberately is to invest his slave chorus with the presence and aura of citizen witnesses. ⟨. . .⟩

The generic slave women of *Choephori* participate in the play with extraordinary power. No other slave chorus in surviving tragedy is remotely comparable, and very few choruses of any kind: the Erinyes, the Danaids, perhaps the Bacchae. How are we to respond to them? We might assert that the *Choephori* chorus essentially act like any other chorus. ⟨. . .⟩

⟨. . .⟩ But why, in that case, does Aeschylus create such a choral force? If the audience does *not* entertain essentially different dramatic expectations from male choruses and female, from free and slave, from old and young, why do these types exist in tragedy at all? It is perfectly true that all choruses have common elements and common generalizing functions. So too do such "characters" as kings and queens, princes and princesses, seers and nurses. But I am not persuaded, to speak only of Aeschylus' choruses, that the Persian elders, the Theban women, the Danaids, the Oceanids, the elders of Argos, the foreign slave women, the Erinyes display more of a common identity than they do their individual characters and specific roles. ⟨. . .⟩

I come, then, to some final tentative thoughts on why Aeschylus composed *Choephori* with this particular chorus. The *Oresteia* is full of bold dramatic moves, nowhere more so than in the choruses. The stories, apocryphal or not, attached to the effects which the first sighting of the Erinyes in *Eumenides* had on the audience are only the most notorious sign of this feature of the *Oresteia*. The dramatic risks to a large extent involve issues of gender and gender roles. Females in the trilogy are powerful, resolute, intelligent, violent; males are regularly hesitant, ineffectual. The Argive elders in *Agamemnon* are easily recognized as timorous and vacillating; a tremendous arc spans the distance between that chorus and the Furies. The slave women of *Choephori* form an uneasy middle between these extremes. They should be more irresolute, more obedient than the male citizen elders, but are exactly the opposite; and yet their female forcefulness, for all its range and intensity, is clearly less than what the audience will experience with the Erinyes. Once *Eumenides* is under way, the progression from ineffectual elders to dominant slave women to awesome female divinities may assume an overall shape to the audience. But during the course of *Choephori* itself, the role of the chorus is intended to unfold as a succession of shocks. We are *not* meant to be comforted by feeling that this choral group could be almost any other; that is impossible. The female slaves, as they control, urge, drive those around them, make us tense and uneasy. They are yet another social element that is not acting within normal constraints. ⟨. . .⟩

—Marsh McCall, "The Chorus of Aeschylus' *Choephori*," in *Cabinet of the Muses: Essays on Classical and Comparative Literature in Honor of Thomas G. Rosenmeyer,* ed. Mark Griffith and Donald J. Mastronarde (Atlanta: Scholars Press, 1990): pp. 23, 25–27.

Plot Summary of the
Eumenides

Although it ends in seeming optimism, the *Eumenides'* darker shadings make it a difficult play to classify. H. D. F. Kitto rightly noted that its arguments had to be absurd: Justice was, after all, a zero-sum game in *Agamemnon* and *Choephori;* and *Eumenides* does not solve, but rather rephrases their moral deadlock. This is why the Furies' conversion seems strained. The god of the machine decrees a celebratory ending to the *Oresteia,* but like civilization itself, that ending is a compromise—and an uneasy one at that.

The action begins with Apollo's priestess, the Pythia, who traces the lineage of Apollo's powers. Preparing to welcome her suppliants, she comes instead upon the Furies, asleep in a circle around Orestes. The Furies could be seen only by their victim in *Choephori,* but in the *Eumenides* they have sprung to vivid and hideous life. Shaken with horror and repulsion, the Pythia declares herself unequal to this pollution: Only the god himself can clear this place.

Apollo duly appears. His obvious, visceral disgust for the "Gorgons" prepares the clash of Olympian and chthonic gods; and he sends Orestes to Athens, where the plague is to be lifted. As Hermes leads Orestes away, the ghost of Clytemnestra appears to rouse her Furies back to the chase.

On finding their quarry gone, the Furies send up an immediate lament. Apollo, a mere "Young god" and "common thief," has violated their just domain, which was to avenge matricide; the world-order is upset, with blood unpaid for. Apollo himself drives the Furies from his temple, trading insults through a dozen lines of stichomythia. The god insists that Clytemnestra's death was just, since her crime had threatened the holiest bond: the marriage of man and wife. After reiterations by all of their determination not to yield, he and the Furies leave the stage.

Orestes has now reached Athens. But the Furies are close behind, and follow his footsteps (much as Electra had in the *Choephori*) until they find him before Agamemnon's shrine.

The Furies initially refuse to submit to a court trial. Their law is simple—an eye for an eye—and permits of no compromise. Yet

Orestes has been purified by Apollo: The madness of *Choephori* is clearly gone, and he brought no stain on those who gave him asylum. The only pollution remaining, in fact, is the Furies' chase, and he calls accordingly for Athena, who alone can release him now. As Orestes prays, the Furies begin their dance, calculated to drive its victims to madness. Their powers, they insist, were allotted by the Fates themselves, and are essential to the very ordering of the world: "So the center holds."

Fresh from Troy, Athena arrives, and the Furies resolve to submit to her judgment: "We respect you. You show us respect." After hearing the case, however, Athena professes herself unable to rule for either party. Instead, she proposes, they will institute a court of law—the first—to try this and all future cases of murder.

As Athena gathers a jury, the Furies begin a new chant, warning that all order is threatened if Orestes goes free: "deathstrokes / dealt by children wait their parents, / mortal generations still unborn." Without terror—called today, fear of the Lord—cities and men cease to be righteous; all morality is contingent on the *lex talionis,* which after all is the only justice the Furies know. It is worth noting that this is no exaggeration of the Furies' importance: Tradition held that the chthonic gods were never subservient to the Olympians, but ordered the universe jointly through a division of labor.

Athena brings her citizen-judges to the Crag of Ares; Apollo also now materializes, and the trial begins.

The Chorus Leader opens the questioning. The facts of the crime are easily stated: Directed by Apollo, Orestes killed his mother to avenge his father. When he asks why, if they are truly agents of retribution, the Furies never pursued Clytemnestra, the Leader answers as she had before: A woman who kills her husband violates no bond of blood. Orestes' reply hints of things to come: "Does mother's blood run in my veins?"

Apollo, testifying for Orestes, reasserts the legitimacy of his act, this time grounding it specifically in the will of Zeus. To this the Leader retorts that Zeus came to power by overthrowing Kronos, and so could hardly be one to speak for a father's rights. The parties are at an impasse—indeed, have been so since the play began. Apollo's insistence is on the unequivocal right of marriage; the Furies', on the unequivocal wrong of matricide. No middle ground is possible, and so Apollo tries an entirely new defense: A mother's womb, he says, serves as merely an incubator for the man's seed. "The father can father forth without a mother" —Athena, after all, came to birth motherless; none ever came to birth fatherless. This teaching was promulgated by Anaxagoras, but it is unlikely Aeschylus believed it himself. Rather, he adopts it to engineer a deliberately ambiguous acquittal, in which neither side may be seen to have held higher moral ground.

Prosecution and defense having completed their arguments, Athena gives her final instructions to the jury. Apollo and the Chorus Leader continue to quarrel as the votes are cast, and are still doing so when Athena announces her vote for Orestes: "No mother gave me birth. / I honour the male . . ." .

The votes are counted, and Athena announces a tie—meaning Orestes goes free. Thanking the goddess at length, and promising an alliance with her city, he departs. And the unsatisfied Furies at once voice their humiliation: "I, robbed of my birthright, suffering, great with wrath, / I loose my poison over the soil, aieee!—" The goddess soothingly reminds them the verdict was no insult—the vote was a tie—and that Zeus himself ordained all this. She asks them to bless the land, promising eternal honors; but the Furies merely repeat the refrain of their lament. So Athena tries again—this time alluding not-so-subtly to the power of Zeus' thunderbolt. With the threat, she as well offers a bribe: prospect of the first fruits, to be reserved to the Furies at ceremonial rites once they consent to her terms.

The Furies are finally persuaded. They will cease civil war and blight, and Athens will rely on them to flourish. The Leader relents: "Your magic is working . . . I can feel the hate, / the fury slip away"; and to initiate them in their role as "kindly goddesses" (though the word "Eumenides" does not appear within the play), Athena teaches them a new song, rite of blessing and fertility. The Furies are to be transformed, rather than exiled or killed: "I enthrone these strong, implacable spirits here," says Athena, "and root them in our soil."

The Furies' delirium grows and spreads, fanned by Athena's encouragements. Themes which had clashed in the *Agamemnon* and *Choephori* find their resolution at last: "the lightning stroke / that cuts men down before their prime, I curse, / but the lovely girl who finds a mate's embrace, / the deep joy of wedded life—O grant that gift, that prize . . . ". Visions of prosperity and fertile abundance replace the murdered virgin Iphigeneia, and the adulteries of Clytemnestra and Helen. And persuasion, which had lured a husband to his death, here reconciles the Furies with the city of Athens.

The Furies are clothed in red, in a visual effect which epitomizes the moral revolution of the play: *Agamemnon*'s blood-red carpets become the Furies' festal robes, their conversion reversing the iniquities of Clytemnestra. The Furies are joined in a procession modeled after the *metoikoi,* or resident aliens, at the annual Panatheneia.

A ritual cry of animal sacrifice (*ololugmos*) was raised over Agamemnon by Clytemnestra, and over Clytemnestra by the libation-bearers; these now yield to hails of triumph, on which the play and trilogy end: "All-seeing Zeus and Fate embrace, / down they come to urge our union on— / Cry, cry, in triumph, carry on the dancing on and on!"

Innocence and guilt have been irrelevant to acquittal, and the Furies' wrath only stayed with bribery and threats. E. T. Owen found harmony in all this; Anne Lebeck found irony. Very likely, Aeschylus intended both.

Philosophy alone could not order a disordered world: As George Thomson observed, the question, "Is a man justified in avenging his father by killing his mother at the command of God?" is after all unanswerable. Tragedy was a political institution, and his use of spectacle to close the *Oresteia* suggests that Aeschylus, too, appreciated the role of art—and artifice—in sustaining a civil society.

The *Eumenides* does not attempt to save us. Rather, it raises a hymn of thanksgiving to that compromise of living which, though human and limited, remains nevertheless the best we have. ✸

List of Characters in the
Eumenides

The **Pythia** is placed at the start of *Eumenides,* immediately elevating it to a divine plane new to the *Oresteia.* Priestess of Apollo, she elaborates the (peaceful) transitions by which the god inherited his powers, foreshadowing the ultimately bloodless incorporation of the Furies into Athena's city.

When the play begins, **Apollo** has put the Furies to sleep. He is both Orestes' partisan and, in a sense, his co-defendant; for it was he who decreed Clytemnestra's murder. Apollo initially argues that the queen violated her pact of marriage (as had Cassandra in *Agamemnon*), but he is eventually to fall back on Anaxagoras' theory of male parentage. His purification of Orestes has not entirely worked.

The messenger-god **Hermes** escorts Orestes on his journey from Delphi to Athens.

Orestes has recovered his sanity and been purified since *Choephori,* but still cannot escape his mother's Furies. He has no qualms about the justice of his act, and his personality is accordingly limited; as Thomas Rosenmeyer remarked of all Aeschylean characters, Orestes is created to perform the acts required of him by the plot. He is shepherded through *Eumenides* by Apollo and Hermes, and acquitted by Athena.

Clytemnestra, the only character with a part in all three plays of the *Oresteia,* appears here as a **Ghost** wakening her Furies back to their task of revenge.

Furies occur in Cassandra's visions ("a dancing troupe / that never leaves,") in *Agamemnon,* and Clytemnestra's Furies haunt Orestes in *Choephori.* Only in *Eumenides,* however, are they finally and fully instantiated as tangible, living creatures in the **Chorus and Leader.** "No other extant tragedy is built, as this one is, around the raging opposition of the chorus to all the characters" (John Herington). Associated with Night, the old goddesses guard their powers jealously. Their conversion, if wholly convincing, would have made up "the only significant change of mind in Aeschylean drama" (Bernard Knox).

Athena, goddess of wisdom, is called upon to resolve the conflict of *Eumenides,* and founds a law court to decide the case. She casts the deciding vote in Orestes' favor, on the grounds that she "[honours] the male, in all things but marriage." When the Furies meet the acquittal with rage, Athena partly threatens and partly bribes them into submission.

The city's **Women** appear to invest the Furies in their new garb of festal robes. Forming a procession with court and audience, they lift the paean of thanksgiving with which the trials of *Eumenides*—and the *Oresteia*—are at last resolved. ❀

Critical Views on the
Eumenides

FRIEDRICH SOLMSEN ON THE AREOPAGUS

[Friedrich Solmsen taught at Cornell University and the University of Wisconsin at Madison. He is the author of *Plato's Theology* (1942), *Aristotle's System of the Physical World: A Comparison with His Predecessors* (1960), and *Isis Among the Greeks and Romans* (1979). Here, he shows how Aeschylus invented the notion of a conflict between two orders of gods, setting up, through the vehicle of Orestes, a dilemma that could only be solved by the civilizing institution of Athena's court.]

⟨. . .⟩ Myth and poetic tradition rather than the sociological realities of contemporary life suggested to Aeschylus the existence of two different orders. Finding the Erinyes embodied in some of the stories of the 'great houses' and their activity implied in other stories of the kind, he would wonder whether the intrinsic difference between their ways and those of the Olympians had to be accepted as a fundamental opposition in the moral universe that could never resolve itself into harmony. ⟨. . .⟩

⟨I⟩t is typical of Aeschylus that while his tragedy has its roots—very strong roots—in the realm of primitive religious beliefs and keeps close enough to these beliefs to bring them into play whenever it seems good, he finds the final solution of his problem in the clearer, and at the same time colder, atmosphere of civic institutions, and with the help of dialectical reasoning.

Without arguments and without hard reasoning there could be no acquittal, and without acquittal there would be no clear sign of the dawn of a new era. If the Areopagus had concurred with the view of the Furies there would still be a new form and procedure of Justice, but unless this Justice won a signal triumph over the old system the power of the new institution would be much less conspicuous.

By giving half of the votes to the Furies—and this after Athena has impressed upon the judges the solemn nature of their decision—Aeschylus indicates that the Justice for which the Furies plead has great significance and cannot be lightly brushed aside. Although Aeschylus has in every possible way emphasized the essentially hideous and repulsive nature of the Furies, he deals fairly and objectively with their mission in the world and their conception of Justice. The equal division of votes represents a maximum of recognition. ⟨. . .⟩

⟨T⟩he other Olympians may have loathed the Erinyes, but they have never questioned the necessity of their work ⟨. . .⟩.

⟨. . .⟩ That the chorus which precedes the trial scene shows the Erinyes so much closer to the mind and outlook of Zeus than any previous one can hardly be an accident, nor should it be interpreted as evidence of what one might call their spiritual growth in the course of the play. The better explanation is that when the decision approaches Aeschylus wishes us to feel that the Erinyes are able to contribute greatly to the realization of a moral order and that an outright repudiation of their claims would entail a real loss of moral values. ⟨. . .⟩

Even in the properly organized city, we have already learned, the factor of dread—⟨*to deinon*⟩—cannot be altogether dispensed with, and the Areopagus should not be considered the only authority that keeps this dread alive in the hearts of the citizens. That the wicked shall not escape punishment is a basic principle of Zeus' government likewise, and whenever his punitive justice is called into action it is almost as unrelenting as that of the Erinyes. Thus once they have been integrated into his order they will make good executives of his supreme will ⟨. . .⟩.

⟨I⟩t is neither from want of skill nor from the absolute lack of an alternative that the glorification of the Areopagus and with it the prospect of a lasting and stable commonwealth begin to claim our attention before Orestes has found his acquittal. Nor again would it be fair to Aeschylus to suggest that he is so fascinated by the political perspective that he loses interest in Orestes. ⟨. . .⟩ By setting forth the mission of the Areopagus in solemn and dignified language, Aeschylus puts us in the frame of mind in which we appreciate the sentence of acquittal as a manifestation of the new civic justice which has found a home in the city state of Athens. ⟨. . .⟩

⟨E⟩ven Zeus and Athena are ready, when they dispense Justice, to resort to the forms and instruments of civil justice; they employ the highest tribunal of Athens for this purpose. By this act they impart to the justice of the city-state a divine quality, yet show at the same time that civic ways of administering justice are worthy to serve as symbols and manifestations of the divine government. It was, after all, in the institutions of the city that the greatest progress in the realization of justice had been achieved ⟨. . .⟩.

—Friedrich Solmsen, *Hesiod and Aeschylus* (Ithaca: Cornell University Press, 1949): pp. 185–86, 195, 199–200, 203, 206, 221–22.

⊗

GEORGE THOMSON ON THE PLAY AND THE CITY

[George Thomson was Professor of Greek at the University of Birmingham. His books include *Studies in Ancient Greek Society* (1949), *From Marx to Mao Tse-tung: A Study in Revolutionary Dialectics* (1971), and commentaries on the *Oresteia* (1938) and the *Prometheus Bound* (1988). In this study (originally published in 1940) he considers the political and social significance of the *Eumenides*, in particular its closing scene.]

To all those critics who have assumed that the question at issue is simply a moral one, the ground on which Athena bases her decision has been a stumbling-block. It would have been easy for the dramatist to make her say that she is going to vote for Orestes out of compassion or humanity (*philanthropía*), because that was one of her traditional qualities; but he has chosen not to base her decision on these grounds, and that makes the grounds on which he does base it all the more significant. And it may well be asked whether there is even an initial plausibility in the assumption which these critics have accepted. Is a man justified in avenging his father by killing his mother at the command of God? If the trilogy had been made to turn on that sterile speculation, they would have been hardly less perplexed than they are now. Æschylus was not interested in the solution of an insoluble conundrum.

The significance of the acquittal is not primarily moral at all but social, and it provides the answer to a question which has been prominent in our minds from the beginning of the trilogy. What is

Justice? Is it the rule of the vendetta? Is it the law of blood for blood? Does it permit of absolution? Does it lie in the act or in the motive? ⟨. . .⟩

⟨A⟩s a Pythagorean, Æschylus was nearer to Hippokrates than to Plato.⟨. . .⟩ Accordingly, asked to define his idea of justice, he would, it may be suspected, have replied in one word—democracy. That answer is implicit in his treatment of the story of Orestes. The matricide is acquitted by an appeal to historical expediency, and the trilogy ends with the ratification of a new social contract, which is just because it is democratic ⟨. . .⟩.

Since the beginning of the century, there had grown up in the city and its environs, attracted by the opportunities of trade, a class of resident aliens (*métoikoi*) whom it was the policy of the government to encourage, although as foreigners they were excluded from civic rights and from the public ceremonies of the state religion. Once a year, however, at the national festival of the Panathenaia, these aliens were not only permitted to take part, but were accorded special marks of honour. The climax of the festival came on the night of the anniversary of Athena's birth, when a robe of saffron, woven by the women of the city, was carried up to the Akropolis in a torchlight procession, led by a band of *épheboi* chosen for the occasion and attended with cries of "Alleluia!" by all the citizens, men and women, old and young, and there hung on the statue of Athena Polias, the goddess of the city-state. In this procession, to mark the purpose of the festival, which was to proclaim peace and good will to all who dwelt under the goddess's protection, the resident aliens were clothed in robes of crimson and attended by a special escort.

The Erinyes have consented to become co-residents with Athena, partakers and joint owners of the soil, and accordingly they now assume the title of *métoikoi,* accepting the goodwill of the citizens and offering their own. ⟨. . .⟩

By his introduction of the Panathenaic procession, the poet has brought his story out of the darkness of antiquity into the brilliant light of the Athens of his day. It began in the remote and barbarous past, it ends here and now. It is as though at the close of the trilogy he invited his audience to rise from their seats and carry on the drama from the point where he has left it.

Of all the features of the *Oresteia,* the most conspicuous is this organic union between the drama and the community out of which it had emerged and for which it was performed—this perfect harmony between poetry and life. In this respect it is almost unique. The audience of the Globe Theatre which witnessed Shakespeare's plays was a cross-section of the community, ranging from the Court to the proletariat, but the audience at the City Dionysia was more than that—it was the community itself, assembled for the performance of a collective ritual act. ⟨. . .⟩

—George Thomson, *Æschylus and Athens: A Study in the Social Origins of Drama* (New York: Haskell House, 1972): pp. 289–91, 295, 297.

⟨⦵⟩

MICHAEL GAGARIN ON SEXUAL CONFLICT AND RESOLUTION

[Michael Gagarin is James R. Dougherty, Jr., Centennial Professor of Classics at the University of Texas at Austin. His works include *Drakon and Early Athenian Homicide Law* (1981) and *The Murder of Herodes: A Study of Antiphon 5* (1989). This extract considers the sexual conflict motivating the *Oresteia,* interpreting Agamemnon's crime as "an offense against marriage from a woman's point of view, committed to reaffirm marriage from a man's point of view." Gagarin has noted that agency continually shifts between male and female (Agamemnon—Clytemnestra—Orestes—Furies), the two being finally reconciled through the intervention of an androgynous god.]

It is ⟨. . .⟩ specifically as a woman that Clytemnestra is wronged, and in the pattern of reciprocity that dominates the trilogy this wrong must be redressed. The crime of man against woman is balanced by that of woman against man, the deceitful (and thus womanly) killing of Agamemnon, husband, ruler, and leader of the military forces. ⟨. . .⟩

⟨T⟩he female dominance in *Agamemnon* is balanced by an even stronger male dominance in *Choephoroi.* ⟨. . .⟩

Orestes brushes off his mother's plea that she nursed him, that she is a true woman in other words, by pointing to her many offenses against marriage from the male perspective: killing her husband, committing adultery, and casting out her son, the proper heir. ⟨...⟩

As in the case of Agamemnon's killing of his daughter, a normally unthinkable deed is justified according to a set of male values that see the crime as less serious than a previous crime against those male values. ⟨...⟩ It is true that Orestes appears to be a less extreme representative of the male point of view ⟨...⟩. ⟨He⟩ is continually aware of the impious nature of his deed, he acts only after much deliberation and persuasion, and he recognizes the need for some sort of payment (purification) for his act. ⟨...⟩ Thus, in spite of the fact that Orestes, like Agamemnon, acts from male values and through his action establishes the dominance of male forces, his is a less extreme act, and the audience may suspect that some sort of compromise is now closer to hand.

An end to the cycle of *drasanti pathein* does not, however, come automatically with Orestes' victory. Clytemnestra's death does not leave her powerless but rather brings on her agents of revenge, the Furies, who appear to Orestes at the end of the play. They are immediately identified as women. ⟨...⟩

⟨T⟩he Furies maintain that Clytemnestra's killing of Agamemnon is less important than Orestes' killing of Clytemnestra, since the latter violated a blood tie but the former did not. In response, Apollo argues the supreme sanctity of marriage, holding up Zeus and Hera as an example. We have already seen that from the male perspective the marriage bond is more highly valued than the blood tie. ⟨...⟩

⟨...⟩ The view that the male is the sole true parent is ⟨...⟩ Apollo's one convincing argument: in reply to it the Furies have nothing to say, and upon it Athena bases her vote for Orestes' acquittal. ⟨...⟩ This final argument is in no way irrelevant; in fact it is directed at one of the central concerns of the trilogy, the clash between male and female forces and values. ⟨...⟩

⟨Athena's⟩ bisexuality seems to give her the ability to act as a neutral arbitrator in the sexual conflict and to persuade the Furies that they were not really defeated. ⟨...⟩

⟨The Furies⟩ threaten to pour out their wrath on the city, but in the end they are appeased and persuaded to grant the city their favor instead. Just as their threatened evil is a barren plague, so their blessing is one of fertility, a feminine blessing to match the masculine contribution of Orestes' promised military alliance. ⟨. . .⟩ The Furies ⟨. . .⟩ agree to prevent men from dying young and to help furnish young maidens with husbands, thereby reestablishing the value of marriage. Male and female elements, which have been in conflict since before the beginning of *Agamemnon,* are thus reconciled at the end of *Eumenides.* Sexual harmony is established at last. ⟨. . .⟩

> —Michael Gagarin, *Æschylean Drama* (Berkeley: University of California Press, 1976): pp. 94, 97–101, 103–5.

ⓑ

Philip Vellacott on Right, Wrong, and the Verdict

[Philip Vellacott is the author of *Ironic Drama: A Study of Euripides' Method and Meaning* (1975), *The Logic of Tragedy: Morals and Integrity in Aeschylus'* Oresteia (1984), and of translations of Aeschylus, Euripides, and Menander of Athens. Like both Rosenmeyer and Lebeck, Vellacott interprets the reconciliation of the Eumenides as ironic or implausible. In this extract, he questions whether the forces of Right do indeed win out in Aeschylus' "happy ending."]

⟨. . .⟩ Aeschylus establishes a single moral canon in three different aspects in the three plays. This canon is not justice. The Elders see no further than justice, nor do the chorus in *Choephori;* the annihilation of Troy, and the two murders, were all just, and Aeschylus shows them all as disastrous crimes. Justice marks the first primitive stage of moral growth, and is in itself inadequate to the needs of a civilized community. It can become constructive only when administered with integrity in a court of inexorable law. The moral values Aeschylus establishes are: in *Agamemnon,* humanity and pity; in *Choephori,* reverence for kindred blood; in *Eumenides,* judicial integrity. In each case he shows human action, willingly or unwillingly, destroying the principle involved. The concept common to all three principles is that of ⟨*aidōs*⟩, which the poet names at the crucial point of the whole action, when Orestes confronts his mother. ⟨. . .⟩

⟨. . .⟩ In *Eumenides* we shall notice that the quality of ⟨*aidōs*⟩, the capacity for horror, has faded, and is replaced by a concern for ritual and legal status. ⟨. . .⟩

⟨. . .⟩ Aeschylus, by presenting the Erinyes in the horrific garb of popular fancy, challenged his audience to recognize moral values under whatever disguise. They failed his test—as, indeed, did Zeus, who, Orestes claimed, judged by appearance ⟨*orōn*⟩. Critics too, both ancient and modern, encouraged by Apollo's intemperate abuse and Athena's patronizing smoothness, have assumed that Aeschylus presents the Erinyes as barbarous and bloodthirsty creatures who are converted by Olympian justice and eloquence to civilized behaviour. (A still more curious distortion of Aeschylus' text sometimes goes unchallenged: the notion that the Erinyes uphold the primitive order of bloody revenge, while Apollo favors trial and conviction by impartial law. This is the opposite of what in fact happens in *Eumenides*.) ⟨. . .⟩

⟨. . .⟩ The heart of the trilogy is its comment on mankind's struggle for moral independence and vision—a comment which becomes specific at *Cho.* 896–903. Once this is perceived, we shall find that after the first two tragedies, *Eumenides* presents not so much a synthesis of old and new traditions as a statement of conflict and a warning of defeat; that Aeschylus presents the trial of Orestes not as a civilized alternative to murderous revenge but as an inadequate and corruptible substitute for a positive and humane moral standard; and that what appears on the surface as a celebration of national unity and confidence is, on a deeper level, an ironic enactment of the most comprehensive tragedy of all, the moral tragedy of Athens. ⟨. . .⟩

The goddess makes no mention of right or wrong, of the needs of a healthy society. She betrays the deterrent principle she has solemnly enjoined on the court. ⟨. . .⟩ Her "principle" moves from the inadequacy of justice not towards an idea of goodness, but towards the interest of a social structure founded on power. ⟨. . .⟩

⟨. . .⟩ The audience is applauding. Presently, after the panathenaic hymn of joy, they will award first prize to Aeschylus. We need not conclude that they approve either murderous revenge or matricide. But they have seen the august court of Areopagus, presided over by Athena, conduct a trial on lines familiar to every one of them from regular jury service, and the proceedings have exemplified every offense against integrity which they condemn in theory but approve in practice—prevarication, intimidation, evasion of issue, bribery; and they recognize all this as normal, and find the verdict acceptable. ⟨. . .⟩

⟨. . .⟩ Athena has silenced the sole voice that insisted on an absolute distinction between good and evil. The defeat of ⟨*aidōs*⟩ on the stage, and the approval of that defeat by the audience, symbolically anticipate, in the poet's prophetic vision, that erosion of general moral standards which within three decades led to the appalling collapse manifested in the events of 427 B.C., and described by Thucydides in. Henceforth the Erinyes will be ⟨*eumenides*⟩, kindly, to those who most need their cruel sternness.

> —Philip Vellacott, "Has Good Prevailed? A Further Study of the *Oresteia*," *Harvard Studies in Classical Philology* 81 (1977): pp. 114–18, 120–21.

⟨♋⟩

D. A. HESTER ON THE VOTE

[D. A. Hester teaches at the University of Adelaide in South Australia. Below, he examines the major arguments made both for and against Athena's having merely tied the vote (as opposed to affirmatively tilting the balance in Orestes' favor).]

⟨. . .⟩ Gagarin argues that the tie *includes* the vote of Athena, who votes twelfth. His basic reasons are:

(1) The voting is accompanied by ten couplets, spoken alternately by the Furies and Apollo, and a final triplet; these eleven speeches provide for eleven voters (so also Kitto); (2) Athena's language strongly suggests that she actually has a voting pebble in her hand. What does she do with it, and how is this displayed on the stage? The simplest assumption is that she puts it in the urn soon after men-

tioning it and before the count starts, so that it is counted with the others; on any other assumption the audience could have been left in doubt about what had happened. ⟨...⟩

These points are less than convincing. In (1) we have to explain the unexpected triplet. It is (perhaps) more likely that it provides for the last juror to vote and retire and Athena to come forward than that it provides for two jurors to vote. But surely it could even more easily provide for no jurors to vote, but for Athena to cross to the voting urns? With respect to (2), I would agree that Athena has a voting pebble in her hand. She emphasizes that it is the last vote and that she will cast it in addition, which language at least seems to leave it open to her not to at once put it in an urn. She is waiting to see if the votes are equal; if not, no responsibility will rest with her. ⟨...⟩

The arguments on the other side are considerably stronger. Verrall points out that Athena expressly disclaimed any intention of deciding the case. Can she now vote to overrule the human jury to which she has entrusted it? Thomson also sees an inconsistency, in which she tells the Furies that they have not really been defeated because the votes were equal. More significant, surely, are the reactions of Orestes and the Furies. If Athena's vote produced the tie, the human votes going against Orestes, we would expect Orestes to be indignant with the Athenians and extremely grateful to Athena; the Furies, on the other hand, would be well disposed to the Athenians and furious with Athena. What do we in fact find? Orestes does indeed express first his gratitude to Athena, as in all courtesy he must, but he continues with an enthusiastic restatement of his promise that his successors will be faithful allies of Athens. The Furies divide their reproaches, between the "new gods" and the Athenians, but are especially heavy on the latter; they do not mention Athena by name. Does this not fit the assumption that the human votes were equal, and Athena gave the casting vote?

Let us try to look at the possibilities as they may have appeared to the dramatist. He wants the cases for and against Orestes to balance. This would suggest an equal vote on the human jury. Orestes must, however, be acquitted. He probably found already established the legal principle that equal votes acquit. This would be hopelessly undramatic. Athena must vote in person as (perhaps) she was already deemed to have symbolically voted in other cases. But if her decisive vote is announced after the equality of human votes has been established, the natural sequel will be for the wrath of the Furies to be turned on her, and the subsequent scene, in which she acts as a mediator between her city and them, will be difficult to stage. No; let her declare her preference for Orestes before the decisive moment, so that it is not clear that her vote will be counted and the immediate wrath of the Furies can be avoided, and let the balance of responsibility rest with the jury, not with her.

She must, however, give a reason, and here there is a difficulty. Will not the reason destroy the balance that Aeschylus has been at pains to establish? Will it not commit him to one side or the other, when neither side can be regarded as altogether right or wrong? This, I would maintain, is the basic reason why her vote is given on personal grounds. She does, it is true, repeat Apollo's argument that the male should have preference over the female, just as ⟨elsewhere⟩, she repeated the argument of the Furies that fear is a necessary element in a civilized state. Although she was used as an example by Apollo to demonstrate that the mother is not a parent, she does not draw this conclusion herself. Rather, she gives the one reason which could never be used as a precedent in any actual trial and thus breaks a deadlock which was on moral grounds insoluble. What juror in the future will ever be called upon to vote who is the direct offspring of Zeus and has never had a mother?

—D. A. Hester, "The Casting Vote," *American Journal of Philology* 102, no. 3 (1981): pp. 269–72.

⟨❦⟩

NANCY S. RABINOWITZ ON THE FURIES' CONVERSION

[Nancy S. Rabinowitz is Professor of Comparative Literature at Hamilton College. She has written *Anxiety Veiled: Euripides and the Traffic in Women* (1993), and co-edited *Feminist Theory and the Classics* (1993). Here, she compares the play with archetypal myths of dragon-slaying, showing how Aeschylus exploits the Furies' dual nature in order to make more believable their incorporation into the life of the city.]

Aeschylus makes it clear in several distinct ways that his Erinyes are representatives of the dragoness. First, they are explicitly identified with Clytemnestra, the dragon enemy of the first two plays. Then, they are linked to the traditional opponents of Apollo in his struggle for Delphi, in his struggle with Dionysos, and in his servitude to Admetos. Finally, they recall other monsters and are given the epithets and characteristics of dragons. ⟨. . .⟩

⟨. . .⟩ While they see themselves justly punishing the evildoer, their mission soon degenerates into simple lust for blood, and their association with blood marks them as monsters who eat their victims for the joy of it. They are as eager to consume their victim as are Lamia, Skylla, Echidna or Keto. ⟨. . .⟩

⟨. . .⟩ The infliction of plagues is as we have seen a weapon typical of dragons; it is associated with the Erinyes in the *Choephoroi* and is threatened in the *Eumenides.* ⟨. . .⟩

⟨. . .⟩ The Delphic scene serves not only to make vivid the challenge of the Erinyes, but also to indicate how it will be met. The hint comes from a new version of the Pythian foundation myth which Aeschylus sets out at once in the Priestess' prologue. Here she recognizes the older and alternative power of Ge, the original prophet of the place, but far from referring to Apollo's battle with Delphyne or Python as the means of his succession, she states that the transfer of authority was accomplished without any violence ⟨. . .⟩.

⟨. . .⟩ The new myth provides a paradigm for Aeschylus' action. For in this final play, Athena and Apollo act not as dragon slayers but as dragon transformers—they work without force. ⟨. . .⟩

⟨. . .⟩ Athena also transforms one of the dragoness' old attributes, since persuasion was Clytemnestra's weapon in the destruction of Agamemnon, and it is the means the Erinyes try to use to bewitch Orestes. ⟨. . .⟩

⟨I⟩t might seem unlikely that they would be susceptible to reason and persuasion; they are rendered approachable, however, by that very duality which characterizes some of their dragon kin. The Erinyes, angry demons who have come to be seen in such black terms, were like Ge once potent for good as well—in fact, it is this dual potency that makes it imperative that Aeschylus work out a way to integrate them into the order he is creating. The dramatist makes the transformation of the Erinyes credible in two ways. First, he establishes a side of their nature which is not foreign to the Olympians. And second, he utilizes the fertility of the dragoness-Erinyes.

While the Erinyes are strongly characterized as monsters, it is also true, as has been widely recognized, that they have a concern for order. In their role as dragonesses they are separated from the Olympians by a wide gulf, but in their role as punishment deities, they approach the gods of Zeus' dispensation. Indeed, in the early sections of the *Agamemnon*, the Erinyes are the agents of Zeus' justice. ⟨. . .⟩

⟨. . .⟩ The central stasimon of the *Eumenides* shows a clear solicitude for the positive values of the *Agamemnon*, and it is this aspect of the Erinyes that Athena depends on and evokes in her successful persuasion.

The inherent duality of the Erinyes may be seen in their threats as well as their promises, for both reflect their connection to nature: as dragoness they can blight, as fertility deity they can bless. When Aeschylus makes the Furies kind, he simply restores to them their double nature and reunites the two facets of the goddess of life and death. The Erinyes' threats, as we have analyzed them, are summarized in Athena's statements of what they must not do. These make a compilation of their dragon capabilities: they should *not* make the land fruitless; *not* poison it; *not* cause men to destroy their own seed. At the same time, the honors she offers them (first fruits) and the promises they then make reflect the ancient fertility connection of the dragoness. In their prayers against storm, etc., the goddesses grant growth and prosperity to crops and mortals, a power which derives from their original double nature. ⟨. . .⟩

⟨. . .⟩ As she instructs the chorus in their new song, Athena touches on all the elements shown as evil in the *Choephoroi* hymn and asks the Erinyes to make them good once again. The transformation and purification of the imagery in each case take an attribute of the dragoness in the earlier plays—dark and false light, storm, plague—and restore it to a positive meaning.

—Nancy S. Rabinowitz, "From Force to Persuasion: Aeschylus' *Oresteia* as Cosmogonic Myth," *Ramus* 10.2 (1981): pp. 179, 181–85.

[Thomas G. Rosenmeyer is Professor Emeritus of Greek and Comparative Literature at the University of California at Berkeley. He is author of *The Masks of Tragedy: Essays on Six Greek Dramas* (1963), *The Green Cabinet: Theocritus and the European Pastoral Lyric* (1969), and *Senecan Drama and Stoic Cosmology* (1989). In this extract Rosenmeyer argues that, despite traditional understandings of his "theodicy," Aeschylus invariably contrived his gods in keeping with the specific needs of a particular plot.]

⟨. . .⟩ Aeschylus does not have his characters or the chorus speak of a conflict between divine wills. The disharmony between Artemis and Apollo is as important to our understanding of *Agamemnon* as is the peculiar authority of Zeus. But the two divinities are not related logically. They operate independently, and when they appear to run afoul of each other, the disturbance is more like an incidental and unforeseen friction than like a systematic confrontation. We learn that Artemis won out, but we are not left with the impression that the victory entailed a defeat for Apollo. Even in the third play, where Apollo and the Furies lock in battle, the deflections arranged for by the rhetoric of the masque refashion what might have been a battle of wills into a serial exposition of independent voices. ⟨. . .⟩ To say that both Apollo and the Furies are symbols may be correct but is not very helpful, for the symbolism is not the same. Apollo is a person, and acts on behalf of another person, Zeus. ⟨. . .⟩ The Furies are more like abstractions. ⟨. . .⟩

From Heraclitus and others, we know that the Furies interest themselves in all irregularities; the philosopher reflects that the Sun cannot overstep his bounds, i.e., deviate from his course, because if he did the Furies, the ministers of Regularity, would find him out and, one suspects, punish him. ⟨. . .⟩ Indeed, in the first two plays of the *Oresteia*, the Furies are always on the side of justice and normalcy—and that means on the side of the Olympians and Zeus. It is only in the final play that, temporarily, because of the needs of the plot, they are converted into adversaries of the celestial legislators, and that is because the Olympians are, at that point, given a new function in addition to their role as patrons of domestic and clan stability: the guardianship of a rule of equity which supersedes the familiar lines of justice. The Furies, in their role as upholders of the old institutions, are thus brought into opposition with the innovators, the younger, freer, unconventional gods: a position not unlike the one in which Prometheus finds himself in *Prometheus*. Like him, the Furies are associated with the Earth and the subterranean powers. They call themselves children of Night. In that capacity, they are removed from human iconography and take on animal shape. Apollo, speaking of the Furies, uses language that recalls the most bizarre formulations of archaic art. Cassandra also refers to them as an irksome throng, drinking human blood, cacophonous, brash. ⟨. . .⟩

But Aeschylus's art sees to it that the Furies are not merely beasts, bogeywomen calculated to frighten enlightened mortals, but not quite managing to do so. They are, after all, the assistants of Right, and Right is at the center of all three plays ⟨. . .⟩. ⟨B⟩lood works autonomously. The Furies themselves acknowledge, in stately dactyls contrasting pointedly with the skewed rhythms before and after, that they have no intercourse with the rest of the gods. They avow that their business is a bloody one; they adopt a civilized tone of revulsion before it. It is important to appreciate the implication of this alleged independence of action; the Furies seek out and punish offenders without reference to the commands of Zeus. This is an ad hoc contrivance. ⟨G⟩enerally speaking nothing is exempt from participation in the total order of Zeus. But as the Furies champion the causes that are endangered by the new institutions and particularly as they defend the cause of women, whose rights the new arrangements are going to restrict, they burn with a spirit of freedom and moral purpose which gains for them an authority far more respectable than that of the argumentative Apollo. ⟨. . .⟩

The shifting nature of the Furies in the *Oresteia* gives us a full measure of the many uses to which Aeschylus can put his divinities. They are ghosts or demons, the crude materializations of a simple terrified faith. But they are also symbols, of varying degrees of concreteness and condensation, cited with an increasing momentum whenever Aeschylus wishes to say something about the conflicting claims of competing and successive social and moral orders. ⟨. . .⟩ What distinguishes the Aeschylean gods is their ease of association, the naturalness with which they inhabit the drama and mesh their purposes with those of men. ⟨. . .⟩ With men, they share a fluidity of design; they live in the text, and the text defines their being. For a critic to construct an Aeschylean theology would be as quixotic as designing a typology of Aeschylean man. The needs of the drama prevail.

—Thomas G. Rosenmeyer, *The Art of Aeschylus* (Berkeley: University of California Press, 1982): pp. 270–71, 281–83.

⟨ɷ⟩

Simon Goldhill on *Dikē*

[Simon Goldhill is a Resident Fellow in Classics at King's College, Cambridge. His books include *Language, Sexuality, Narrative: The Oresteia* (1984), *The Poet's Voice: Essays on Poetics and Greek Literature* (1991), and *Foucault's Virginity: Ancient Erotic Fiction and the History of Sexuality* (1995). Here, he shows the *Oresteia* to be a contest over the language of *dikē* (which can variously mean "justice," "retribution," "penalty," or "court," among other things)—each character struggling to gain control by defining the word according to his own perspective.]

Kitto comments 'if Dikē conflicts with Dikē . . . the universe is chaotic and Dikē cannot yet be "Justice". ' The next line in the text, however, which Kitto does not quote, reads 'O gods, be just in what you bring to pass'. The gods are exhorted to bring things to pass 'in a just way' (*endikōs*), that is, an appeal is made to precisely the ordered, general standard of Justice, Right, that the previous line was quoted to show as utterly lacking. The chaos of conflict is not the neatly ordered opposition of Right to Right, as Kitto maintains, so much as the juxtaposition of a line proclaiming the clash of *dikē* and *dikē* to a line maintaining a criterion of judgement for that clash which is constructed in the same vocabulary. ⟨. . .⟩

⟨. . .⟩ After the matricide, as he stands over the bodies of his mother and her lover, Orestes calls on the Sun to be a witness to his actions. His speech, like Agamemnon's first lines, reverberates with the language of *dikē*:

> . . . be a witness for me in my day of trial
> how it was in all right I achieved this death,
> my mother's: for of Aegisthus' death I take no count,
> he has his seducer's punishment, no more than law.

I have quoted Lattimore's translation for the build-up of untranslatable puns in these lines. The expression 'in my day of trial' is *en dikēi*, '*in dikē*', 'in court', 'in the case'. Here *dikē*, particularly juxtaposed to the term 'witness', seems to stress a precise legal context—indeed, to look forward to the trial of the *Eumenides*. The word translated 'in all right' is *endikōs*, an adverb formed from *en* and *dikē*, and it is in the same metrical position as *en dikēi* in the previous line. It's as if the adverb could be seen as broken into its parts. But the adverb *endikōs* has the connotations of a general standard of justice, right, rather than the institution of the law court that was suggested by the phrase 'be a witness *en dikēi*'. The term for Aegisthus' punishment is *dikē* also. ⟨. . .⟩

As Orestes feels himself becoming less and less stable, he turns once more to justification in terms of *dikē*:

> While I am still in my wits, I say publicly to my friends:
> I killed my mother not without some right . . .

The double negative of 'not without *dikē*' seems to emphasize Orestes' claim to right, but at the same time to mark the effort to repress the possibility that the matricide was an act committed 'without *dikē*'. But what could be a sufficient translation for *dikē* in this expression? It recalls all the senses of 'retribution', 'penalty' and 'justice' that have been at play, as well as the legal implications of the forthcoming trial.

What these two passages indicate is that for the reader or audience there is a double movement involved in the dynamics of *dikē* in this trilogy. ⟨. . .⟩

This double movement can be seen well in Orestes' two speeches. In the second, Orestes claims *dikē* for his action: 'I killed . . . not without *dikē*.' He asserts his justification for matricide through the term *dikē*. But the first speech's triple repetition of *dikē* and its cognates in a wide range of contexts and implications remains in a significant tension with the claim of Orestes. Can Orestes avoid suggesting the legal implications of murder, the possibility of his own punishment, the lawcourt to come? In other words, for the reader or spectator, even when a character utters a strong claim to have *dikē* on his or her side and seems to stress a particular implication of the term, the network of meanings in the text involves that claim in a series of further implications and connotations. 'In the language of the tragic writers there is a multiplicity of different levels . . . this allows the same word to belong to a number of different semantic fields depending on whether it is a part of religious, legal, political or common vocabulary or of a particular sector of one of these. This imparts a singular depth to the text and makes it possible for it to be read on a number of levels at the same time.' Thus, as we saw to be the case in numerous expressions, the boundaries between respective domains of meaning remain opaque and cannot be clearly and rigidly delimited in the complex, reverberating repetitions and echoes of the text. It is both such depth of signification and the role of the clashing rhetorics of appropriation that are suppressed in a reading which supposes a secure and ordered transition from vendetta to law in the language of *dikē* in the *Oresteia*.

—Simon Goldhill, *Reading Greek Tragedy* (Cambridge: Cambridge University Press, 1986): pp. 42, 45–47.

Works by Aeschylus

Surviving plays:

Persae [*The Persians*], 472 B.C.

Hepta epi Theobas [*Seven Against Thebes*], 467 B.C.

Hiketides [*Suppliants*], ca. 463 B.C.

Oresteia, 458 B.C.:

    Agamemnon

    Choephori

    Eumenides

Prometheus desmotes [*Prometheus Bound*], date unknown

Lost plays:

in a tetralogy with the *Seven Against Thebes:*

    Laius

    Oedipus

    Sphinx (satyric)

in a tetralogy with the *Suppliants:*

    Egyptians

    Danaids

    Amymone (satyric)

Proteus (satyr-play of the *Oresteia* tetralogy)

Lykourgeia tetralogy:

    Edonians

    Bassarids

    Neaniskoi [*Youths*]

    Lycurgus (satyric)

Other plays believed to have been authored by Aeschylus:

Alcmene

Argives

Argo

Atalanta

Athamas

Award of Armor

Bacchae

Bone-Gatherers

Builders of the Bridal Chamber

Cabiri

Callisto

Carians [Europa]

Cercyon

Champions at Isthmia [satyric]

Children of Heracles

Circe (satyric)

Conjurers of the Dead

Cretan Women

Cycnus

Eleusinians

Epigoni

Etnaeans

Eurytion

Glaucus the Sea God

Heliades

Heralds

Huntresses

Hypsipyle

Iphigenia

Ixion

Lemnians

Lion

Memnon

Myrmidons

Mysians

Necromancers

Nemea

Nereids

Net-Drawers

Niobe

Nurses

Orithyia

Palamedes

Penelope

Pentheus

Perrhaebians

Philoctetes

Phineus

Phercides

Polydectes

Priestesses

Processional

Ransom of Hector

Semele

Sisyphus (there may have been two plays by this name)

Telephus

Tenes

Toxotides

Weighing of Souls

Women at Aetne

Women of Salamis

Xantriai

Works About
Aeschylus

Aristophanes. *The Frogs.* Tr. Richmond Lattimore. Ann Arbor: University of Michigan Press, 1962.

Bowie, A. M. "Religion and Politics in Aeschylus' *Oresteia.*" *Classical Quarterly* 87.1 (1993): 10–31.

Chiasson, Charles C. "Lecythia and the Justice of Zeus in Aeschylus' *Oresteia.*" *Phoenix* 42.1 (1988): 1–21.

Crane, Gregory. "Politics of Consumption and Generosity in the Carpet Scene of the *Agamemnon.*" *Classical Philology* 88.2 (1993): 117–36.

Davies, Mark I. "Thoughts on the *Oresteia* Before Aischlos." *Bulletin de Correspondance Hellénique* 93.1 (1969): 214–60.

Dawe, R. D. "Inconsistency of Plot and Character in Aeschylus." *Proceedings of the Cambridge Philological Society* 189.9 (1963): 21–62.

———. "The Place of the Hymn to Zeus in Aeschylus' 'Agamemnon.'" *Eranos* 64 (1966): 1–21.

Dodds, E. R. "Morals and Politics in the Oresteia." *Proceedings of the Cambridge Philological Society* 186 (1960): 19–31.

Dover, K. J. "The Political Aspect of Aeschylus' *Eumenides.*" *Journal of Hellenic Studies* 77.2 (1957): 230–37.

Dyer, R. R. "The Evidence for Apolline Purification Rituals at Delphi and Athens (Plates II–V)." *Journal of Hellenic Studies* 89 (1969): 38–56.

Edwards, Mark W. "Agamemnon's Decision: Freedom and Folly in Aeschylus." *California Studies in Classical Antiquity* 10 (1977): 17–38.

Finley, John H., Jr. *Pindar and Aeschylus.* Cambridge: Harvard University Press, 1955.

Fraenkel, Eduard, ed. *Aeschylus, Agamemnon.* 3 vols. Oxford: Oxford University Press, 1950.

Gagarin, Michael. "The Vote of Athena." *American Journal of Philology* 96.2 (1975): 121–27.

Garvie, A. F. "The Opening of the *Choephori.*" *Bulletin of the Institute of Classical Studies of the University of London* 17 (1970): 79–91.

Golden, Leon. *In Praise of Prometheus: Humanism and Rationalism in Aeschylean Thought.* Chapel Hill: University of North Carolina Press, 1962.

Haldane, J. A. "Musical Themes and Imagery in Aeschylus." *Journal of Hellenic Studies* 85 (1965): 33–41.

Havelock, Eric A. *The Greek Concept of Justice: From Its Shadow in Homer to Its Substance in Plato.* Cambridge: Harvard University Press, 1978.

Herington, John. *Aeschylus.* New Haven: Yale University Press, 1986.

————. "The Influence of Old Comedy on Aeschylus' Later Trilogies." *Transactions of the American Philological Society* 94 (1963): 113–25.

Jones, John. *On Aristotle and Greek Tragedy.* London: Chatto & Windus, 1962.

Kitto, H. D. F. *Poiesis: Structure and Thought.* Berkeley: University of California Press, 1966.

Knox, Bernard M. W. "The Lion in the House (*Ag* 717–36 [Murray])." *Classical Philology* 47 (1952): 17–25.

Lawrence, Stuart E. "Artemis in the *Agamemnon.*" *American Journal of Philology* 97.2 (1976): 97–110.

Lebeck, Anne. "The First Stasimon of Aeschylus' *Choephori:* Myth and Mirror Image." *Classical Philology* 57.3 (1967): 182–85.

————. *The Oresteia: A Study in Language and Structure.* Washington: Center for Hellenic Studies, 1971.

Lesky, Albin. *Greek Tragic Poetry.* Tr. Matthew Dillon. New Haven: Yale University Press, 1983.

Lloyd-Jones, Hugh. "The Guilt of Agamemnon." *Classical Quarterly* 12.2 (1962): 187–99.

Macleod, C. W. "Politics and the Oresteia." *Journal of Hellenic Studies* 102 (1982): 124–44.

Moritz, Helen. "Refrain in Aeschylus: Literary Adaptation of Traditional Form." *Classical Philology* 74.3 (1979): 187–213.

Müller, C. O. *Dissertations on the Eumenides of Aeschylus.* London: John W. Parker, 1853.

Nietzsche, Friedrich. *The Birth of Tragedy, and the Case of Wagner.* Tr. Walter Kaufmann. New York: Vintage Books, 1967.

Quincey, J. H. "The Beacon-Sites in the *Agamemnon*." *Journal of Hellenic Studies* 83 (1963): 118–32.

Rose, Herbert Jennings. "Theology and Mythology in Aeschylus." *Harvard Theological Review* 39.1 (1946): 1–24.

Rosenmeyer, Thomas G. *The Art of Aeschylus.* Berkeley: University of California Press, 1982.

———. "Gorgias, Aeschylus, and 'Apate.'" *American Journal of Philology* 76.3 (1955): 225–60.

Seaford, Richard. "The Last Bath of Agamemnon." *Classical Quarterly* 78.1 (1984): 247–54.

Simpson, Michael. "Why Does Agamemnon Yield?" *Parola del Passato* 137 (1971): 94–101.

Smith, Peter M. *On the Hymn to Zeus in Aeschylus'* Agamemnon. Chico: Scholars Press, 1980.

Solmsen, Friedrich. "Strata of Greek Religion in Aeschylus." *Harvard Theological Review* 40.4 (1947): 211–26.

Stanford, W. B. *Greek Tragedy and the Emotions: An Introductory Study.* London: Routledge & Kegan Paul, 1983.

Stoessl, Franz. "Aeschylus as a Political Thinker." *American Journal of Philology* 73.2 (1952): 113–39.

Sutton, Dana F. *The Greek Satyr Play.* Meisenheim am Glan: Hain, 1980.

Taplin, Oliver. "Aeschylean Silences and Silences in Aeschylus." *Harvard Studies in Classical Philology* 76 (1972): 57–97.

———. *The Stagecraft of Aeschylus.* Oxford: Oxford University Press, 1977.

Vermeule, Emily. "The Boston *Oresteia* Krater." *American Journal of Archaeology* 70 (1966): 1–22.

Vidal-Naquet, Pierre. "Hunting and Sacrifice in Aeschylus' *Oresteia.*" In *Tragedy and Myth in Ancient Greece,* eds. Jean-Pierre Vernant and Pierre Vidal-Naquet, 150–74. Tr. Janet Lloyd. Sussex: Harvester Press, 1981.

Vickers, Brian. *Towards Greek Tragedy: Drama, Myth, Society.* London: Longman, 1973.

Index of
Themes and Ideas

AESCHYLUS, biography of, 13–15

AGAMEMNON, 16–43; Aegisthus in, 17, 18, 20, 22, 25, 30, 41; Agamemnon in, 10–11, 12, 14, 15, 16, 17, 18, 19, 21, 23, 24, 27, 28, 29, 30, 32, 33–35, 36–37, 38, 39, 40, 41–43, 55, 76; and Agamemnon's inherited guilt, 17, 30, 41–43; and Agamemnon's murder as echo of Clytemnestra's, 44, 47, 57–58, 59–60; and Agamemnon's surrender in carpet-scene, 18, 33–35, 37; and carpet-scene and robes of Furies in *Eumenides,* 25–26; Cassandra in, 10–12, 16, 18–19, 21–22, 24, 28, 30, 36, 39, 42, 54, 55; characters as agents of transition in, 39–41; characters as images in, 35–37; characters in, 21–22; and *Choephori,* 44; Chorus in, 16–17, 18–20, 22, 25, 27, 28, 33, 40, 55, 64; Clytemnestra in, 10–12, 14, 16, 17, 18–20, 21, 28, 30, 34, 36, 37–39, 40, 42, 55, 76; Clytemnestra's language in, 18, 36, 37–39; corruption in, 16; critical views on, 23–43; dance in, 14, 23–24; *dikē* (just) in, 16, 19; Electra in, 10; Furies in, 16, 19, 62, 64, 84, 85; Herald in, 17, 21, 36; and imagery implying Agamemnon's guilt, 31–33; Iphigeneia in, 15, 16, 17, 18, 19, 23, 27–28, 30, 32, 33, 42, 43; language of sacrificial slaughter in, 27–28; line-by-line exchanges in, 55, 59; lion cub in, 14, 18, 27–28, 54; nature in, 37–38; Orestes in, 10, 12, 18; plot summary of, 16–20; as psychological drama, 44; sexual conflicts in, 12, 17, 19, 21, 37, 76, 78; and time, 29–30, 39–40; Watchman in, 16, 21; Zeus in, 12, 14–15, 17, 32, 38

CHOEPHORI, 44–65; Aegisthus in, 45, 46, 47, 49, 51, 53, 57, 58, 63, 88; Agamemnon in, 44, 45, 46, 47, 50, 51–52, 53, 54, 56, 57, 77; and alienation from Clytemnestra, 52–54; blood in, 25, 26; characters in, 48–49; and Chorus and intimations of drama's catastrophe, 63–65; Chorus and Leader in, 44, 45, 46, 47, 48, 50–51, 52, 53, 56, 57–58, 61, 63–65, 78; Cilissa in, 46, 49, 54, 58, 63; Clytemnestra in, 40, 44, 45, 46, 48, 51–54, 57, 58, 59–60, 63, 77; and Clytemnestra's murder as echo of Agamemnon's, 44, 47, 57–58, 59–60; critical views on, 50–65; *dikē* (just) in, 50, 87–88; Electra in, 18, 44–45, 46, 48, 50, 51, 52–53, 55, 56, 57, 63, 66; Furies in, 45, 47, 61–62, 66, 77, 83, 85; invocation in, 44, 45–46, 50–52, 56, 57, 63; line-by-line exchanges in, 45, 54–56, 59; moral values in, 78–79; myth in, 53–54, 57–58; Orestes in, 14, 43, 44, 45, 46–47, 48, 50, 51–52, 54, 55, 56, 57, 58, 59, 60–62, 63–64, 77, 87–88; Orestes' madness in, 47, 60–62, 63–64; plot summary of, 44–47; Porter